Ki
Solomons
Temple

BY

E. RAYMOND CAPT M.A., A.I.A., F.S.A. Scot.

Archaeological Institute of America

COVER DESIGN AND ORIGINAL ILLUSTRATIONS BY J. A. DRYBURGH

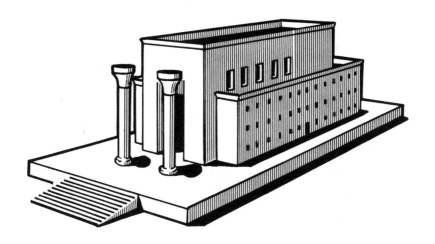

PUBLISHER

ARTISAN SALES
P.O. Box 1529
Muskogee, OK 74402
Phone (918) 682-8341

ISBN 0 - 934 666 - 05 - 9
Library of Congress catalog card number: 79 - 54774

1

MAP OF THE

HOLY LAND

in the

TIME OF DAVID

THE
TWELVE TRIBES.

I.   Judah.
II. Simeon.
III. Benjamin.
IV. Dan.
V.   Ephraim.
VI. Manasseh.
VII. Issachar.
VIII. Zebulon.
IX. Asher.
X.   Naphtali.
XI. Gad.
XII. Reuben.

Scale of Eng. Miles.

35 Longitude East from Greenwich 36

2

PREFACE

The Temple of Solomon, known as the House of God was, in some respects, the most wonderful building constructed by human craft. The Biblical reference of the Temple conveys to the reader, its grandeur and holiness, but reveals so few details that little hope was held of ever producing an accurate reconstruction.

Many attempts in the past to reconstruct the Temple have produced a wide variety of sketches and plans, some of them fantastically imaginative.

Modern archaeologists, seeking to shed light on the Bible's most famous building, have dug amid the ancient masonry of Mt. Moriah or Temple Hill in Jerusalem, and searched for parallels and origins in contemporary buildings in Egypt, Mesopotamia and Phoenicia. (Canaan)

Their discoveries have revealed the architectural skill and building power of Solomon and his successors. Not only has the accuracy of the Sacred Scriptures been confirmed, but we can more vividly visualize the buildings, decorations and furnishings of the Temple.

Today, a visitor to Jerusalem can see the very stones placed in position by the masons of Solomon. He can explore the ingenious system by which water was brought to the Temple Hill and stored there. He can enter the great cavern under the Old City, now known, with some justification, as Solomon's Quarries where the famous white limestone that formed the basic building material of the Temple was cut and finished by Phoenician craftsmen.

In recent years, several conceptions of Solomon's Temple have been published. The Howland — Garber model, a work incorporating most recent discoveries, is in the opinion of this writer, the most realistic presentation to date. Linear illustrations of this reconstruction are shown in this work.

This booklet is designed to bring you a brief study of the Temple and a better understanding of its spiritual meaning.

NINETEENTH CENTURY ENGRAVING OF JERUSALEM BY MOONLIGHT

WHY WAS IT BUILT?

"In the beginning, God created the heavens and the earth."

The Scriptures speak of God as a "wise Master Builder," and of his laying the "cornerstone" of creation. Because God is the builder of this and other worlds, Masonry calls Him the Supreme Architect of the Universe. Hence, architecture is as old as the universe.

When God, the Supreme Architect of the Universe wanted an earthly house or temple, in which to dwell among men, he gave to men the plan of the building he would have them build.

A temple means a great house. In a higher sense it means a house of worship. In the highest, it means a habitation of God. Since God, whom, *"the heaven, and the heaven of heavens cannot contain,"* (II Chron. 6:18) is spirit, why did He approve of Man's construction of a house or temple?

The answer plainly is: because men are prone to forget God: To lose the sense of God's nearness. Because men are forever losing this sense, it must be constantly restored. If man was completely spiritual he would need no temple, no forms of worship. He would see God in all places and feel His presence at all times. But since man has fallen, it is only through forms that God can guide us up to a higher spiritual condition or restoration.

If it were not for the visible world in which we live, God would be nothing to us. Yet God would exist just as he does now. It is through the visible creation that the invisible God becomes a reality to us. The building of the Wilderness Tabernacle was an effort of God to bring men nearer to Him through material forms. Man is so material in his nature that immaterial truth must be put into material forms before he can understand it.

God is not in one place more than another, but men must be made to feel that He is somewhere, before they realize that He is everywhere. Because of this demand in human nature, God appointed men to build the Tabernacle, which was but an allegory, a figure for the time then present till... *"a greater and more perfect Tabernacle, not made with hands, that is to say, not of this building."* (Heb. 9:11)

Solomon's Temple was built in answer to man's need of a sacred place of worship. Not that it was to become more sacred than other places, it was only declared so through an impressive ceremony, to aid men in realizing the sacredness of all places.

God teaches us that material things are sacred in the same way. He takes a part of the things He has made and sets them apart for a sacred use. In doing so, He teaches us all things are sacred, because everything is made by Him and everything God made is very good. (Gen. 1:31) God made man, therefore, man is, in his essential nature, sacred. But man has lost the sense of his own sacredness. Now, God would restore this lost sense.

SYMBOLISM IN THE TEMPLE

The Scriptures in many places employ ideas borrowed from architecture to convey to the mind of man, spiritual and heavenly things. The good man is called a "living stone," a "spiritual house," "God's building" and a "temple of the Holy Spirit."

The House of God, known as Solomon's Temple, also used architecture to convey spiritual truths. No Biblical scholar will venture to deny that in its construction and mode of building can be found an apparent design to establish a foundation for symbolism.

As in the Tabernacle, each detail of the Temple's construction, from the foundation to the roof, embodied a symbolism, in forms, to teach men spiritual truths. Each holy vessel, garment and covering, every substance, its texture, color, sound or odor — everything pertaining to sensory perception was symbolic of some particular aspect of Messianic truth proclaimed for the edification of mankind.

The importance of the Temple symbolism is shown in the amount of attention given to it in the Bible. A large part of both the Old Testament and the New Testament is taken up with this symbolism. It is often referred to by the prophets, the apostles and even by Jesus Christ.

Since the history of the Temple is a part of the Bible, is not its symbolism a part of the Bible? Should not every stone and piece of timber have a meaning to us? We should search. We are invited to do so: *"It is the glory of God to conceal a thing: but the honor of kings is to search out a matter."* (Prov. 25:2)

The glory of the Temple and its services (which were shadows of better things to come) have passed away, but its symbolism gives us a glimpse, in prophetic vision, of a new creation, when *"old things are passed away; behold, all things are become new."* (II Cor. 5:17)

A study of the symbolism of this holy structure will not only lead us to the "Lord of the Temple" but reveal a truth hidden by the infinite wisdom of the Almighty for illumination in this day; to remove the "blindness" from our eyes.

Solomon's Temple in its glory and splendor symbolizes man in his original pristine state of being; a temple, which the "indwelling Spirit," illuminated and hallowed. But this temple was undermined by sin, and has become a sad ruin. As we should expect, a man stands a contradiction to nature. Sin has rendered him unnatural. He is manifestly in a state in which some accident has left him. In a word, man is fallen, a temple "crumbled and ruined;" Like Zerubbabel's Temple, the Fire of the Holy Spirit extinguished.

Can he be restored? Is man, the temple of the Holy Spirit, to remain a ruin forever? No; God made man, therefore, man is, in his essential nature sacred. The Word of God has gone forth, the promise has been given, that on the site of its ruin it may rise again, a goodly structure. By the skillful hand of the "Master Builder," the foundation was laid and the design restored. This is the central theme of the Bible, in which can be found the plans of the living Temple God would have each man build.

The EMPIRE of DAVID

HISTORY OF THE TEMPLE

The Temple originated as a thought in the mind of David. In the second Book of Samuel we read how King David was given rest from all the enemies of his kingdom and began to think it wrong that he should enjoy residence in *"an house of cedar, but the Ark of God dwelleth within curtains."* (II Sam. 7:2; I Chron. 17:1)

Nathan the Prophet agreed with the king and told him to go ahead and do something about it. God guided the hand of the king in writing out the full and complete plans for the construction and furnishings of the Temple he would have built. *"All this, said David, the Lord made me understand in writing by his hand upon me, even all the works of this pattern."* (I Chron. 28:19)

But before David's plans had matured, God told David of a different plan. Although he would be allowed to plan and gather materials, David would not be allowed to carry out the erection of his desired house of God. Because David had been a *"man of war"* and had *"shed much blood,"* (I Chron. 22:8; 28:3) his son, a man of peace (which is the meaning of the name Solomon) would be assigned the task. (I Chron. 22:9,10)

David, now prohibited from building a Temple for the Lord, began to collect and prepare the material for its erection by Solomon, his son, a self-imposed task to which David devoted his declining years. The site chosen for the Temple was Mt. Moriah, one of the several hills rising out of a mountain ridge known as Mt. Zion. Much of the history of this famous site is related in the Bible. Genesis twenty-two records how Abraham prepared to sacrifice his son Isaac on this hallowed ground.

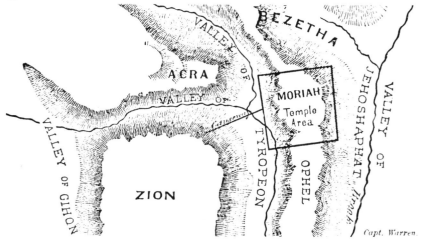

9

The second Book of Samuel, chapter twenty four relates how King David bought Mt. Moriah from a Jebusite named Araunah, who owned a threshing floor on its summit, for 50 shekels of silver. David wanted to build an altar to give thanks for the end of a pestilence that had killed 70,000 men of his kingdom. David in giving thanks said, *"This is the house of the Lord God."* (I Chron. 22:1) So we see that even before the Temple was built, the site was called the "House of God."

The site of the threshing floor lies today within the sacred enclosure of the Moslems known as the Haram esh-Sherif ("Noble Sanctuary"). The most striking natural feature is a great outcropping of rock some 58 feet long, 51 feet broad and 4 to 6½ feet high. This is known as es-Sakhra or the "Sacred Rock" and today is covered by the structure called the "Kubbet es-Sakhra." ("Dome of the Rock") The "Sacred Rock" shows indications of having been used as an altar in very ancient times. Cut channels on the surface of the rock can still be traced that appear to have served as conducts for the blood of sacrificial animals, to an opening on the top of the rock and on to a cavity below.

While the rock itself may have served as Araunah's threshing floor, it is more likely the relatively large and level area directly east of the rock would have provided a better surface for the work of threshing, and became the site of David's altar. This level site would also have been the logical site of Solomon's Temple with perhaps the Holy of Holies situated directly over the rock. Some scholars suggest the "Altar of Burnt Offerings" was constructed over or alongside of the rock, the latter location being more probable; the rock with its underground chamber accommodating the blood of the sacrificial animals. Underground conduits carried the blood to the nearby Valley of Kidron.

After the death of David, Solomon began the noble task of erecting the Temple which his father had planned. Solomon sent word to Hiram, King of Tyre: *"And behold, I purpose to build an house unto the name of the Lord my God, as the Lord spake unto David my father, saying, Thy son, whom I will set upon thy throne in thy room, he shall build an house unto my name. Now therefore command thou that they hew me cedar trees out of Lebanon; and my servants shall be with thy servants: and unto thee will I give hire for thy servants according to all that thou shalt appoint: for thou knowest that there is not among us any that can skill to hew timber like unto the Sidonians."* (I Kings 5:5,6)

THE CEDARS OF LEBANON — 1873 ENGRAVING

CUTTING CEDARS FOR THE CONSTRUCTION OF SOLOMON'S TEMPLE

Hiram, King of Tyre replied: *"I have considered the things which thou sentest to me for: and I will do all thy desire concerning timber of cedar, and concerning timber of fir. My servants shall bring them down from Lebanon unto the sea: and I will convey them by sea in floats unto the place that thou shalt appoint me..."* (I Kings 5:8,9)

RELIEF FROM PALACE OF SARGON II
SHOWING PHOENICIAN SHIPS TOWING LOGS OF CEDARWOOD

The mountains of Lebanon provided the major source of cedar in Bible times. Growing to a height of over one hundred and fifty feet, cedars of Lebanon (cedrus libani) were regarded as the stateliest of trees (I Kings 4:33) and symbols of strength and power. (Psalm 92:12) They were the most sought after and highly prized trees in the ancient world.

RESTORATION OF TEMPLE OF SOLOMON BY MORDON

In addition to the material, Phoenician workmen, skilled in wood and metal work, were hired to oversee Solomon's workers. It is also intimated that Hiram, the renowned mason king, sent stone masons to cut, square, hew and polish the stones for the sacred edifice. Solomon also employed Hiram, the widow's son, an accomplished Tyrian artist.

The widow's son, also known as Ab. Hiram or Hiram Abiff (Father Hiram), was made the chief architect in the construction of the Temple. He is described in the Bible as *"a man full of wisdom and understanding and cunning."* (II Chron. 2:13) His father was a citizen of Tyre, a worker of brass, while his mother was of the tribe of Dan, and apparently a widow of a man of the tribe of Naphtali. Thus he was by birth partly Hebrew and partly Phoenician.

The work on the Temple was begun in the fourth year (974 B.C.) of Solomon's reign and finished in the eleventh, a little over seven years. Its completion was the elevation and the purification of the national faith. The Commandments of Moses were studied, and followed with scrupulous care. All the general sacrifices, to be provided by the head of the nation, were regularly offered. The three great festivals of the year were now, for the first time, regularly observed, and the ordinance of David as to the course of the priests and Levites was now set in motion, it being distinctly recorded that this was done as David, had commanded. (II Chron. 8:12-16; I Kings 9:25)

Solomon died in 926-25 B.C. and was succeeded by his son Rehoboam. The strained relations between the northern tribes and the monarchy gave way to open revolt and the division of the United Kingdom of Israel came to pass. From the building of the Temple by Solomon, Jerusalem, though always accounted to the tribe of Benjamin, became more or less inter-tribal. It became the Mecca for all Israel until the division of the kingdom, after which the tribe of Judah asserted a right to the "holy city."

Judah's claim to the city of Jerusalem may have come about due to the fact that the Judean territory terminated at the southern gates of the city. The throne of Judah on Mount Zion in so close proximity to Jerusalem and the coronation of the royal kings taking place in the Temple in Jerusalem may also have contributed to the validity of any claim made by the royal tribe of Judah. In any case, Jerusalem became the frontier capital of the southern group known as the Southern Kingdom of Judah as opposed to the Northern Kingdom of Israel.

For nearly four centuries after the division of the kingdom, Solomon's Temple continued to serve the people of Jerusalem. During this time a succession of kings followed Rehoboam; the Northern Kingdom of Israel together with a large number of the people of the

RELIEF FROM PALACE OF SENNACHERIB AT NINEVEH SHOWING CAPTIVES OF NORTHERN KINGDOM OF ISRAEL BEING CARRIED AWAY TO ASSYRIA

Southern Kingdom of Judah, were taken captive to Assyria; (Jerusalem alone of the major cities of the south successfully resisted the Assyrians) the Babylonians conquered the Assyrians; and Jehoiachin became King of Judah. (cir. 598-597 B.C.)

"Jehoiachin was eighteen years old when he began to reign, and he reigned in Jerusalem three months...At that time the servants of Nebuchadnezzar king of Babylon came up against Jerusalem, and the city was besieged. And Nebuchadnezzar king of Babylon came against the city, and his servants did besiege it. And Jehoiachin the king of Judah went out...and the king of Babylon took him...And he carried out thence all the treasures of the house of the Lord and the treasures of the king's house... And he carried away Jehoiachin to Babylon... And the king of Babylon made Mattaniah his father's brother king in his stead, and changed his name to Zedekiah." (II Kings 24:8-17)

BABYLONIAN CHRONICLE OF CAPTURE OF JERUSALEM

From a cuneiform tablet found in the excavations of ancient Babylon, comes this account of the events described in the Bible: "In the seventh year, in the month of Kislev (Nov./Dec.) the King of Akkad (Babylon) assembled his army, and after he had invaded the land of Hatti (Syria-Palestine) he laid siege to the city of Judah and on the second day of the month of Adar (corresponding to the Christian calendar — March 16, 597 BC) he siezed the city and captured the king. (Jehoiachin) He appointed in his place a king (Zedekiah) of his own choice, received rich tribute and sent them to Babylon."

Less than ten years after Nebuchadnezzar set up Zedekiah as a puppet king, the Judeans revolted against Babylon again. Nebuchadnezzar again invaded Judah with his armies, destroying every major city and annihilated most of the population. His army besieged Jerusalem for a year and a half before famine-weakened defenders surrendered to be taken captive to Babylon. After the city was plundered by the Babylonians it was destroyed including Solomon's Temple. Much of the glory of the Temple had already been torn away and paid as tribute when foreign conquerors menaced Judah.

DESTRUCTION OF JERUSALEM BY NEBUCHADNEZZAR

Jeremiah's account of the fall of Jerusalem is given in his 39th chapter. Its epitaph was written by Jeremiah: *"And he hath violently taken away his tabernacle, as if it were of a garden: he hath destroyed his places of the assemble:...The Lord hath cast off his altar, he hath abhorred his sanctuary, he hath given up into the hand of the enemy the walls of her palaces; they have made a noise in the house of the Lord, as in the day of a solemn feast."* (Lam. 2:6,7)

It is very remarkable that the Prophet Jeremiah in his 52nd chapter, in the midst of reciting appalling disaster to Judah and to the Temple, seems suddenly concerned with the symbolic import of the pillars. He even stops his tale of woe to give a graphic description of their singular height and dimensions. Jeremiah goes on to relate the breaking up of the columns, and of their removal by the soldiers of the Babylonians.

Other than just relating the destruction of the pillars, Jeremiah does not appear to be greatly disturbed. Such an attitude would be consistent that the Prophet was given a prophetic vision of the glories of the "last days" and that he beheld the fulfillment of God's covenants and the resitution of Israel in her "appointed land" and the continuation of David's Throne, as symbolically proclaimed by the pillars. Perhaps he saw the Temple, although being destroyed, rebuilt in a new and greater manifestation.

Even though not a stone of Solomon's Temple has been found (even the huge platform it rested on was ruthlessly destroyed by Herod the Great's reconstruction centuries later), by correlating the Biblical descriptions (I Kings chapter 6) with information obtained through excavations in a number of sites in Phoenicia, it is today possible to reconstruct Solomon's Temple with considerable more accuracy than fifty years ago.

There was a period of about 50 years from the destruction of the Temple (by the Babylonians) to the beginning of reconstruction (by Zerubbabel). Through the Prophet Haggai, the Lord encouraged Zerubbabel in his rebuilding with a promise, *"the glory of this latter house shall be greater than of the former."* (Haggai 2:9)

The general plan of this second Temple was similar to the first, but it exceeded the original in almost every dimension by one-third. The first far surpassed it in decorations of gold and other ornaments. Also said to have been missing in the second Temple was the "Ark," the "Urim and Thummin," the "Fire From Heaven," the "Divine Presence" or "Cloud of Glory," and the "spirit of prophecy" and "power of miracles."

RESTORATION OF TEMPLE OF ZERUBBABEL BY CHIPIEZ

Zerubbabel's Temple was often defiled in the wars before Christ, and from time to time additions and changes were made. Notable was the fortifying of the Temple by the high priest Simon II, a practice continued by the Hasmoneans.

Herod's Temple was not the construction of a third Temple, but only a restoration and extensive enlargement of the second. For grandeur and beauty its Greco-Roman architecture exceeded that of the Temple of Solomon. Herod began his reconstruction in 20 B.C. and completed it about a year and a half later. However, subsidiary construction continued up to the time of its destruction by the Romans, under Titus, in 70 A.D.

Herod the Great, who desired to kill the Child Jesus of Bethlehem (Matt. 2:16) had unknowingly prepared the Temple to receive the Lord Christ. The "glory of this latter house" did become "greater than the former" as the latter was hallowed by the presence of the Lord Jesus Christ as the prophet Haggai had foretold to Zerubbabel.

This was also the fulfillment of the words of the prophet Malachi to the priests of Zerubbabel's time, concerning the coming of the Messiah. *"Behold I will send my messenger, and he shall prepare the way before me: and the Lord, whom ye seek, shall suddenly come to his temple, even the messenger of the covenant, whom ye delight in."* (Malachi 3:1)

In 132 A.D. (under Bar Cocheba revolutionaries) the Temple of

Herod was partially restored but three years later Hadrian destoyed it and rebuilt a temple dedicated to Jupiter Capitallnus. The Holy Hill was neglected until the coming of the Mohammedan power to Jerusalem and the completion of the famed "Dome of the Rock," in 689 A.D. It is today the third holiest shrine for Moslems.

The Crusaders turned it into a Christian Shrine in 1099 A.D., renaming it Templum Dominum (or Temple of the Lord). When Saladin captured Jerusalem in 1197 A.D. the Golden Cross was hurled down from the top of the Dome and the Crescent restored.

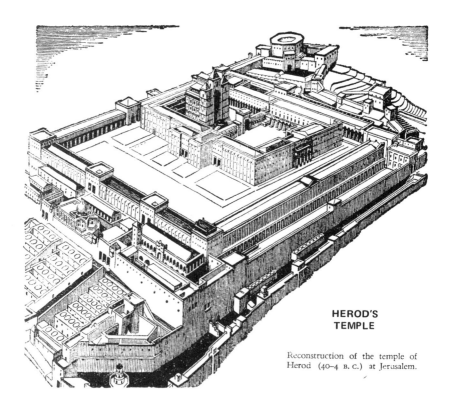

HEROD'S TEMPLE

Reconstruction of the temple of Herod (40–4 B. C.) at Jerusalem.

PLAN OF THE TEMPLE

"Now these are the things wherein Solomon was instructed for the building of the house of God. The length by cubits after the first measure was threescore cubits, and the breadth twenty cubits. And the porch that was in the front of the house, the length of it was according to the breadth of the house, twenty cubits, and the height was an hundred and twenty: and he overlaid it with pure gold...And he made the most holy house, the length whereof was according to the breadth of the house, twenty cubits, and the breadth thereof twenty cubits: and he overlaid it with gold, amounting to six hundred talents." (II Chron. 3:3,4,8)

When King David wished to replace the Tabernacle with a more permanent building, God again furnished the plans of the building He would have built. This plan was communicated first to King David; and David communicated the same to his son Solomon, who took due notice thereof, and governed himself accordingly.

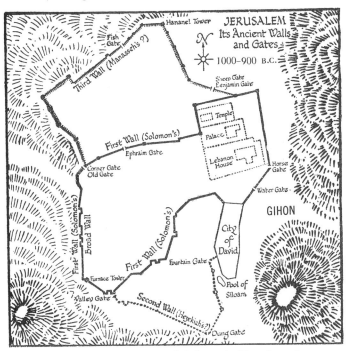

Probable Arrangement of Solomon's Temple and
Palace Buildings.

The Temple was surrounded by two Courts: an "inner court," and a "great court." (I Kings 6:36; 7:12) Their size is not known. The great court may have included the Palace buildings.

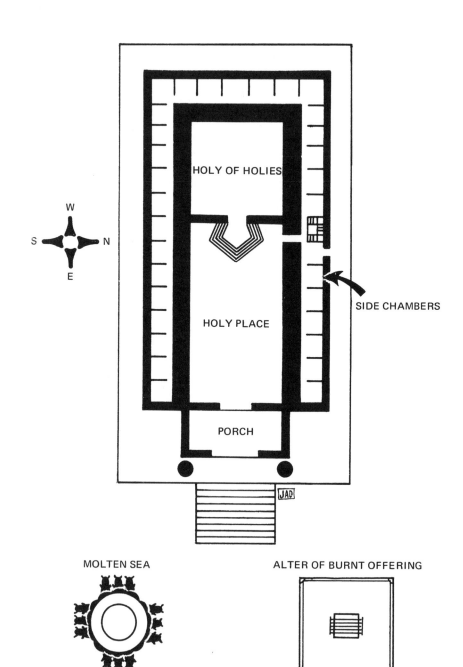

HOLY OF HOLIES

HOLY PLACE

SIDE CHAMBERS

PORCH

JAD

MOLTEN SEA

ALTER OF BURNT OFFERING

FLOOR PLAN SOLOMONS TEMPLE BY R. CAPT

24

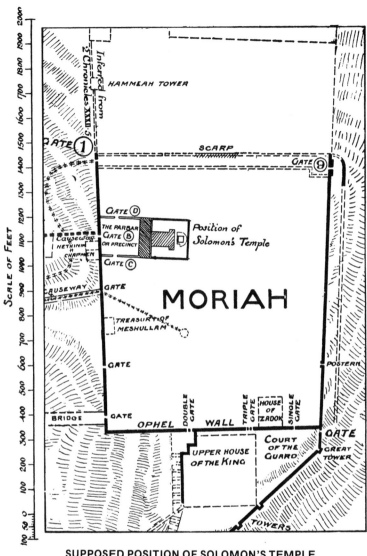

SUPPOSED POSITION OF SOLOMON'S TEMPLE
(SOME LATER CONSTRUCTIONS ARE ALSO SHOWN)

Basically, the Temple was a simple house of two rooms, arranged lengthwise, with a roofed porch protecting the entrance. The interior size of the building is given as 60 cubits long, 20 cubits wide and 30 cubits high.

The "porch" or "vestibule," 20 cubits wide, corresponding to the inside width of the rest of the structure, was 10 cubits deep. Two brass pillars stood on the porch, one on each side of the doorway.

Beyond the porch was the main room known as the "Holy Place," 40 cubits long. Beyond that was the "Holy of Holies," a room in the shape of a cube, 20 cubits in each dimension.

Around the outside of the building were structures described as "side chambers" and arranged in three stories, the ground width being 5 cubits. No adequate information is given to conclude how access to the side chambers was gained, or how the staircase between floors was designed.

I Kings 7:12 describes a wall of "three rows" (or courses) around the Temple Courtyard. It is probable that the Temple walls and raised platform were laid in such fashion. This was characteristic of the Phoenician style of masonry current in that period, as indicated by a part ashlar wall uncovered in excavations at Samaria.

In the court, in front of the Temple, stood the great Altar of Burnt Offerings and the great brass bowl of water called the Molten Sea. On each side of the Temple were five brass Lavers.

In succeeding the Wilderness Tabernacle, the Temple of Solomon preserved and enhanced much of its predecessor's allegory. On comparing the Temple (as described in I Kings 7 and II Chron. 2 and by Josephus 7:3) with the Tabernacle, the first thing that strikes us is that all the arrangements were identical, and the dimensions of every part were exactly double those of the preceding structure.

Thus, the Holy of Holies in the Tabernacle was a cube 10 cubits each way; in the Temple it was 20 cubits. The Holy Place was 10 cubits wide by 20 cubits long and 10 cubits high in the Tabernacle; in the Temple these dimensions were exactly double. The porch in the Tabernacle was 5 cubits deep; in the Temple it was 10. Its width in both instances being the width of the house. The chambers around the Tabernacle and the Temple were each 5 cubits wide, on the ground-floor. The difference was that in the Temple the two walls taken together made up a thickness of 5 cubits, thus making 10 cubits for the chambers.

Taking all these parts together, the exterior ground plan of the Temple measured 80 cubits by 40; that of the Tabernacle measured 40 by 20. The walls were 20 cubits high in one and 10 cubits high in the other. By doubling all the former measurements (of the Tabernacle) then multiplying length by width by height we obtain the volumne of the Temple, which is eightfold greater than that of the Tabernacle. Eight (or octave) is the number symbolic of the beginning of a "new order." The Temple of Solomon prophetically pointed toward a New Order, in the future.

KING SOLOMON'S QUARRIES

"And the house when it was in building, was built of stone made ready before it was brought thither: so that there was neither hammer nor ax nor any tool of iron heard in the house, while it was in building." (I Kings 6:7)

The stone used in the construction of Solomon's Temple came from quarries under the city of Jerusalem. One of the "Royal Quarries" was rediscovered, quite accidentally by an American physician, Dr. Barclay, in 1854 while walking with his two sons and his dog around the city walls. The scent of a fox caused the dog to begin to dig into a hole in the dirt at the base of the wall. Suddenly the dog disappeared and Barclay enlarged the hole uncovering the entrance to an enormous cave.

Later that evening, after being equipped with lamps, a compass and writing material, Barclay and his sons entered the cave. Immediately upon entering, it became evident that the dirt had been piled up intentionally at the opening so as to hide it. This could have been done by the Turks after their rebuilding of the walls of the city in 1542. Going in, Barclay records, they came to a chamber with a high, arched ceiling supported by crude, massive pillars. A twisted path led down into the interior, to additional chambers with whitish ceilings and flat floors. They measured and eagerly recorded the details of the cave unfolding before their eyes.

CHAMBER IN ZEDEKIAH'S GROTTO

INTERIOR OF ZEDEKIAH'S GROTTO
SHOWING ROOF SUPPORTING COLUMNS

28

The opening to the cavern is some 300 feet northeast of the Damascus Gate. It is known today, as "Zedekiah's Grotto" because of the legend of Zedekiah (last king of Judah) fleeing through the cave to a secret opening in the plain of Jericho. This was during the conquest of Jerusalem by the Assyrians in the summer of 587 B.C. The Bible tells in Kings 25:4,5, as well as in Jer. 52:7,8: *"The King with all the men of war fled by night by the way of the gate between the two walls, by the king's garden, though the Chaldeans were around the city. And they went in the direction of Arabah. But the army of the Chaldeans pursued the king, and overtook him in the plains of Jericho; and all his army was scattered from him."* It should be noted, however, the Biblical account does not seem to agree with the location of the cavern.

Zedekiah's Grotto is one of the largest and most extensive man-made caverns in Israel, measuring nearly 750 in depth, and more than 3,000 feet in circumference. Although the entrance is very small, the opening quickly widens into a very wide chamber that slopes down to various branches of the cavern. The various chambers are separated by broad columns left by the quarrymen to support the ceiling. Cut into the walls of the cavern are triangular niches, intended to hold lamps to light up the cavern for the workers.

The rock through which the quarry extends is white massif limestone locally called "Melekeh" or "Royal." Although it is not too hard, it does not flake off easily and after being worked and exposed to the air, turns a characteristically light-pinkish color and becomes much harder. The stone at the opening of the quarry consists of a different stone, also white, but a denser limestone locally called "Mizzi-helou," meaning "Sweet."(soft) It is very easily worked, though its striations prevent its being used in large blocks. There are also other limestones in the cavern bearing iron — "Mizzzi-ahmar" (red) and other harder stones too hard for cutting — "Mizzi-yehudi."(Jewish)

Everywhere can be seen evidence of the methods used by King Hiram's skilled stone masons in hewing the stone. Broad perpendicular cuttings or incisions were cut along a rock face. They were from three to six inches wide and seem to have been made by means of some sort of a pick with a long handle. When made to a required depth, dry wooden wedges were driven into the slits. Water poured over the wedges causing the timber to swell so that the pressure cracked the stone, along the slits. This same method was used by the builders of the Great Pyramid in Egypt.

Here and there, one can see stones half cut still adhering to the side walls. The marks of the pick and chisel are so clear and fresh in appearance that one has little difficulty in imagining that King Hiram's skilled quarry-men are still engaged in cutting the stones, and have only retired from the quarry for their noon-time meal. Several large quarried stones lie as they were left by the workers.

At the end of a small corridor that leads off from the main chamber may be seen a well or basin, about 5 feet in diameter and 2½ feet deep, scooped out of the rock. It is designed to collect and hold water that percolates from fissures in the roof and the limestone walls. Fragments of pottery scattered about the area suggest the water may have been used for drinking purposes by the workers although it is very bitter.

DRIPPING SPRINGS CHAMBER

In one of the chambers the French scholar Charles Clermont-Gannear found a drawing on the wall of a winged sphinx in Assyrian style. It was removed and is at present in the Louvre in Paris. On another wall is seen a carved compass and a builder's angle — masonic symbols. The Freemasons used this chamber for their secret meetings. On the walls and ceilings of all the chambers can be seen traces of rockfalls which occured at various times.

There is reason for supposing that the subterranean caverns, spacious though they be, are only a part of the original quarry. The rugged rock, fifty feet high, on which the city wall now stands, seems to have been scarped not only for defense but early as a rock-cut excavation for building stone. At a distance of about 500 feet, looking north, is what appears to be a "counterscarp". The intermediate space between the scarp and counterscarp is covered with a vast accumulation of rubbish, such as stone chippings over which passes the present road outside the city walls. This rubbish is from 50 to 100 feet in depth which indicates the entire area was at one time an immense quarry. A quarry of such size could easily have furnished the stone for all the Temples of Solomon, Zerubbabel and Herod; the gigantic walls of the Haram, as well as the walls encompassing the city.

Since I Kings 6:7 states that the stones used in the construction of Solomon's Temple were *"made ready before"* being brought to the Temple site, the vast accumulation of stone chippings just outside the quarry suggests that the great stones were dressed there by the masons before leaving the quarry area. As the quarry is quite close to the Temple Hill, it would have been quite easy to transport the huge stones to the construction site. The development of the quarry and the size of the quarry and the size of the stones reflects several Biblical passages:

"And Solomon had three score and ten thousand that bare burdens, and fourscore thousand hewers in the mountains; Beside the chief of Solomon's officers which were over the work, three thousand and three hundred, which ruled over the people that wrought in the work. And the king commanded, and they brought great stones, costly stones and hewed stones, to lay the foundation of the house" (I Kings 5:15-17).

The symbolism of the preparation of the stones and the construction of the Temple in silence is allegorical of man in his process of regeneration,'' which is lifting the soul up out of the degenerate condition into the spiritual condition.

Each of us is a "rough ashlar" or stone like those found in the darkness of the quarry. After being removed from our natural surroundings, we must be "shaped" and "polished," symbolical of moral discipline and training which inspires new practices and new principles. We are then perfected in character through the cleansing of the Spirit before becoming a part of the spiritual Temple.

Dead stones are squared and polished from without, through the use of the mallet, chisel and square, as were the great stones in the walls of the Temple. But men are "living stones" as expressed by the Apostle Peter, *"Ye also as lively stones, are built up a spiritual house, an holy priesthood, to offer up spiritual sacrifices, acceptable to God by Jesus Christ"* (I Peter 2:5).

Living stones are squared, polished and beautified from within. In this work our own efforts are required. But, just as Solomon's masons followed the plans of the Master Builder, we too must follow the direction of the Wise Master Builder. Only by voluntarily following and working out the designs for our life can we become a part of the spiritual house.

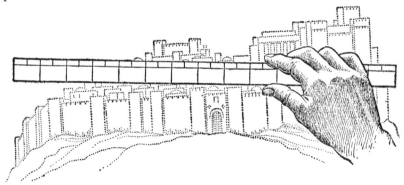

THE FOUNDATION

"And the foundation was of costly stones, even great stones, stones of ten cubits, and stones of eight cubits." (I Kings 7:10)

Ancient temples were built on a raised platform to provide a firm foundation in a soil lacking a rock base. As Solomon's Temple was built on an old rock threshing floor a stone platform was therefore unnecessary. For this reason, some scholars believe the Temple building was flat on the court pavement.

Ezekiel's visionary Temple of the Millennium, in some respects comparable to Solomon's Temple, portrays a platform of 6 cubits high, necessitating a flight of 10 steps to reach the porch. Since Talmudic writings also make mention of stairs, the prevailing theory is the Temple was raised, in keeping with the prevailing style.

In order to provide a courtyard for the Temple, walls were built up from the sides of the mountains, and inside them, all spaces were filled up with earth. At the northeast corner of the Temple area, the wall extends 110 feet below the present level of the ground.

About fifty yards from the front of the "Golden Gate" a shaft was sunk, by the Engineers of the Palestine Exploration Fund (founded 1865) to solid rock, some eighty feet below the present surface. A gallery was then driven up the face of the rock toward the Temple area. When about 50 feet from the Sanctuary wall and 50 feet below the surface, the Engineers came upon a massive masonry wall. It was built in courses, and the stones are large, each course being two and a half feet high and the stones for the most part five feet long. The hard limestone blocks have marginal drafts (narrow borders along the edge of the stones) and rough faces projecting six inches. The horizontal joints are a foot apart, and the space is filled up with six-inch cubes welded together with a cement compounded of red earth, oil and lime. The masonry was pierced by the Engineers for five feet, but there appeared no sign of perforating the entire thickness of the wall.

At the southeast corner, excavations by the Engineers, traced the wall down 79 feet to bed-rock. The wall rises 77 feet above the ground at this point, making the total masonry 156 feet high. The stones discovered forming the foundation are from 4 to 20 feet long and some are 38 feet in length, and about 4 to 6 feet in height.

The foundation corner stone at the south-east corner was found by the archaeologists to measure 14 feet long and nearly 4 feet high. Its function was not only to support the masonry above, like the other foundation stones, but it had to face both ways, forming a bond or union between two walls. The block is described as squared and polished.

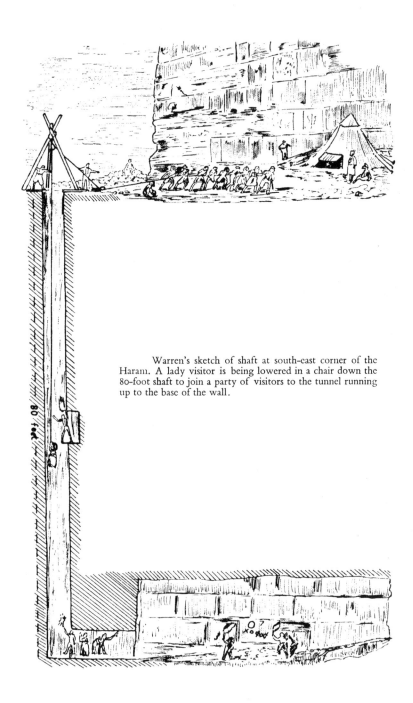

80 foot

Warren's sketch of shaft at south-east corner of the
Haram. A lady visitor is being lowered in a chair down the
80-foot shaft to join a party of visitors to the tunnel running
up to the base of the wall.

It was also noted the foundation rock was comparatively soft for 27 inches, and the cutting for the base of the corner stone was continued for 5 inches more into the hard rock. Fixed in its abiding position nearly three thousand years ago, the great corner stone still stands sure and steadfast, a fitting emblem of the "Rock of Ages."

The second course is more than four feet high, and has proved of much interest, from the existence of painted and incised characters found on the faces of the stones. The first stone is more than 10 feet long, with an ordinary draft at the bottom, but a narrow draft of one inch at the top. The second stone, about 5 feet long, has a broad draft of about nine inches at the top, but only a narrow draft at the bottom. It has a well-dressed face, and near the center was found an incised character, cut about half an inch deep, resembling our letter "H "

INCISED CHARACTERS

The third stone of the course has proved to be the most interesting, from the numerous marks on its face. It has no draft at the top, but a broad draft of about 17 inches at the bottom. On it are seven letters of characters, some of them five inches long. They are painted with red paint, apparently vermillion, and they seem to have been put on with a brush. They are irregularly distributed over the stone.

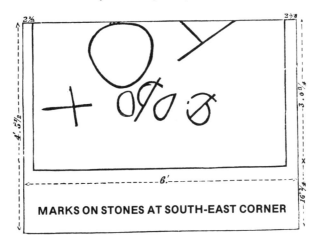

MARKS ON STONES AT SOUTH-EAST CORNER

The trickling of some paint, from a letter on the third stone, was found above the letter itself which certainly could not have happened had the mark been painted on the stone after it was placed in position. This would indicate that the marks were painted, on the stones by the workmen in the quarry.

About three feet from the angle of the cornerstone a hole was found cut out of the native rock, one foot across and one foot deep. It was filled with dirt, which on being cleared away revealed a small clay jar. It was standing in an upright position and had evidently been placed there for some purpose. There were no marks or special features on the jar but it resembled the common pottery of ancient Egypt. Being placed near the lowest corner stone suggests it had something to do with the ceremony of laying the foundation stone.

In patriarchal days, prophets, priests, and kings were set apart for God's service by being anointed with holy oil. The Tabernacle also, and all its furnishings, were consecrated to God by being anointed with the holy oil. In one instance, the Bible records, a stone (Jacob's Pillar) was anointed with holy oil. While, however, there is no direct evidence to its use, it is a reasonable assumption that it did contain holy oil and was used for the consecration of the corner stone, to indicate that the foundations were set apart for the service of the living God.

At 41 feet from the southeast corner, northward, the bed-rock rises abruptly, and here the first course ceases, while the second course becomes partially imbedded in rock. The third course is about four feet high, and is set back four inches. The fourth course is three and one-half feet in height, with a shallow draft of nine inches above. The courses above are for the most part similar to those described, many also containing paint marks on them.

An analysis of the "writings," either painted or cut into the stones, by the Palestine Exploration Fund came to the following conclusions: "First: The signs cut or painted were on the stones when they were first laid in their present places. Secondly: They do not represent any inscription. Thirdly: They are Phoenician." The report considered them to be partly letters, partly numerals, and partly special mason's or quarry signs. Some of them were recognized at once as well-known Phoenician characters. Similar marks have been found in tombs, and stone buildings throughout Phoenicia, dating about the time of Solomon.

The Phoenician alphabet is believed to be the oldest Semitic alphabet in the world. It was used by the ancient Hebrews, as may be seen in the Siloam inscriptions dating about 600 B.C. The ancient letters had an angular script, and continued in use until the Babylonian captivity. The present square (Aramaic) Hebrew characters began to be employed after the exile.

These large foundation blocks have beautifully executed marginal drafts, and the faces are finely chiselled, while the joints are so close that no cement was required. It was noted that marginal drafts and the projecting edges of the faces had been dressed with an eight-toothed chisel one inch wide. The chisel marks are intersected by others at right angles, forming what is called the criss-cross pattern. This mode of dressing is never found in Byzantine work, and, as far as Palestine is concerned, confined almost exclusively to the ancient work of Solomon's time.

The foundations of the massive walls formed the theme of the Psalmist's poetry when he proudly sang of Jerusalem, *"her foundations are upon the holy hills."* Solomon, who probably watched the laying of the foundation stone, expresses the symbolism of the foundation in his Book of Psalms when he wrote, *"the righteous is an everlasting foundation."*

The Bible abounds in interesting allusions to the ''corner stone.''; The Prophet Isaiah, when speaking of the kingdom of God to be established under the new dispensation, exclaims, *"Behold, I lay in Zion for a foundation a stone, a tried stone, a precious corner stone, a sure foundation."* (Isa. 28:16)

God is often called a rock in the Scriptures, *"The Lord is my rock,"* and *"Who is a rock save our God."* The same thought reappears in the Book of Hebrews. *"He looked for a city which hath foundations, whose builder and maker is God."* (Heb. 11:10)

Since God is Truth, then it follows that the solid rock upon which Solomon's Temple is built symbolizes the Truth upon which a man builds his spiritual house; the true Temple of God.

JERUSALEM

37

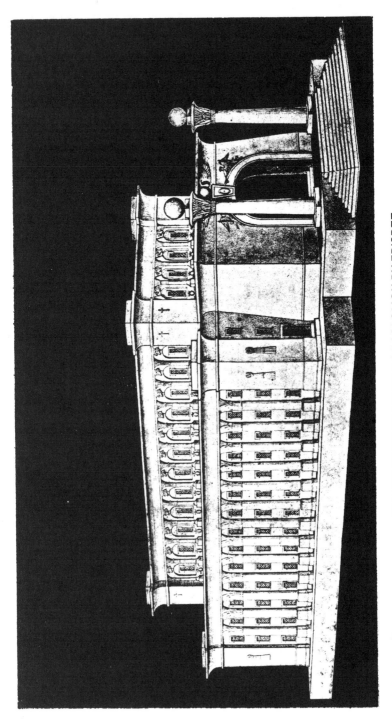

RESTORATION OF TEMPLE OF SOLOMON BY FRISBEE

THE PORCH

"And the porch before the temple of the house, twenty cubits was the length thereof, according to the breadth of the house; and ten cubits was the breadth thereof before the house." (I Kings 6:3)

Solomon's Temple was entered from the east through the Porch, variously translated, from the Hebrew, as "porch;" "vestibule;" "portico" or "entrance hall."

The Scriptures leave the impression it was not considered as an interior room, having no mention of doors as in the case of the main room and the inner Sanctuary. This interpretation is confirmed by the fact that in the record of Kings, reference to the Temple mentions the Holy Place and the Holy of Holies only, excluding the Porch as one of the Temple rooms.

If not considered a part of the "House," the Porch may not have received the wood panelling inside, as did the main rooms. It may have been finished off in stone, as was the outside of the Temple. It seems Solomon's architect wanted to show only stone on the outside of the Temple walls and only wood on the inside. *"And he built the walls of the house within boards of cedar, both the floor of the house, and the walls of the ceiling: and he covered them on the inside with wood and covered the floor of the house with planks of fir."* (I Kings 6:15)

Certain models of the Temple show the Porch as a part of the Temple interior, panelled with cedar of Lebanon, with flooring of fir, but without the elaborate trim and decoration of the rest of the Temple.

The height of the Porch is not given in the book of Kings, but it can be assumed it was not greater — it may have been less — than that of the Temple proper. The statement in II Chron. 3:4 that it was 120 cubits high seems to rest on a corrupt text. It is called a "porch." If it had been 120 cubits high, its title would have been more properly termed "tower." It is very unlikely that, had it been of such height, it would have been overlooked in the book of Kings.

The large entrance was without doors (as evidenced by an inscription found dated at the time of Solomon). The opening is believed to have been approximately 15 feet wide and over 30 feet high, as was the estimated height of the doorway into the main room. This great height was suggested as necessary to accommodate the prefabricated flooring pallets when they were raised on edge and moved into place, inside the Temple.

The opening from the Porch into the main room of the Temple

was provided with a pair of folding doors, of fir, (I Kings 6:34) which had hinges of gold. (I Kings 7:50) As was the practice of the time, it is assumed the doors swung on metal pivots, set in stone sockets.

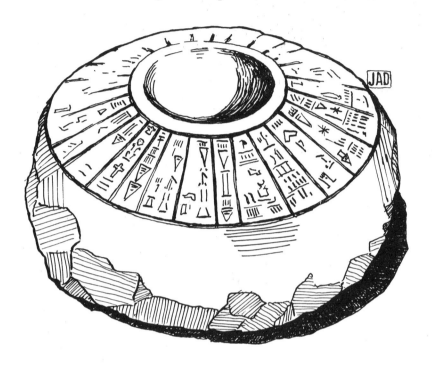

The above inscribed limestone socket (in which a door was pivoted) was found in excavations at Tell Asmar. On the exposed surfaces, of the socket, can be seen words of dedication.

The hinges were of some kind of copper or iron strap, either "overlaid" or "inlaid" with gold, which fastened the doors to the pivots. The hinges could not have been "pure gold" as they would have been too soft to support the estimated weight of the doors.

Early reconstructions of Solomon's Temple show a side room at each end of the Porch, for which there is no Biblical justification. Windows are also often shown in the Porch, but again, without Scriptural reference.

THE TWO PILLARS

"For he cast two pillars of brass, of eighteen cubits high apiece; and a line of twelve cubits did compass either of them about.

And he made two chapiters of molten brass, to set upon the tops of the pillars: the height of the one chapiter was five cubits, and the height of the other chapiter was five cubits:

And nets of checker work, and wreaths of chain work, for the chapiters which were upon the tip of the pillars; seven for the one chapiter, and seven for the other chapiter.

And he made the pillars and two rows round about upon the one network, to cover the chapiters that were upon the top with pomegranates; and so did he for the other chapiter.

And he set up the pillars in the porch of the temple: and he set up the right pillar, and called the name thereof Jachin: and he set up the left pillar, and called the name thereof Boaz." (I Kings 7:15-21)

Among the structural architecture and decoration of Solomon's Temple at Jerusalem, none have exerted more interest and conjecture than the two pillars known as Jachin and Boaz, which occupy so conspicuous a position in the Temple. Their size, shape, height, decoration and above all, their use, meaning, purpose and symbology have given rise to much research, examination and suggestion.

Early authorities on the construction of the Temple once thought of the pillars as having supported the roof of the Porch, but from accumulated contemporary evidence, archaeologists now agree that they were free-standing, and had no structural function. Instead they were only decorative and unquestionably symbolic.

Although I Kings describes the two pillars as castings of "brass," it is more likely they were of copper because brass is a highly impure metal and very easily tarnished. Bronze is also a mixed metal, though less impure than brass, but equally artificial. In a sacred, symbolical Temple, where pure gold was so commonly used, it is highly improbable and inconsistent that any impure artificial metal should be used.

Moses also said that the hills of Palestine contained "copper." (Deut. 8:9) The A.V. renders this as "brass" which of course is artificial and thus could not be found in any mine. Ferrar Fenton translation says "copper." Since the A.V. is clearly wrong in this case, it is probably also wrong in calling the pillars "brass."

Jeremiah 52:21 indicates the pillars were "hollow" which would indicate they were probably highly decorated, copper covered, wooden pillars. From excavations at Khorsabad and elsewhere, castings of copper alloy plates have been found that were made to be fastened to some kind of wood beams or posts. Thus it would have been within the capacity of Solomon's workers to produce such a work.

Some scholars have suggested the two pillars were spiral. This would be in keeping with the numerous spiral examples found in Hebrew columns, both in buildings and sculptured tablets dating back to around 580 B.C. (Zoroaster's tablets) If so, the right-hand column (Jachin) would have had the spirals turning to the right; the left-hand column (Boaz) having the spirals turning to the left.

On top of the pillars there were chapiters that may have served as braziers for the burning of incense or oil. If so, they may have suggested to the worshipper the "pillar of cloud" by day, and the "pillar of fire" by night, which the Israelites knew in the wilderness. (Exodus 13)

The Book of Kings does not mention bases for the pillars but we may assume they had bases because columns, contemporary with and having proportions similar to the Temple pillars, have been found in excavations in Palestine and Syria.

Solomon called the pillars, "Jachin" and "Boaz." (II Chron. 3:17) The exact meaning of these names is not clear but it has been suggested they were key words in some kind of motto invoking the blessings of God on David's Dynasty.

However, it is an established fact that in Solomon's day, named pillars served as perpetual witnesses to solemn covenants. The two pillars undoubtedly represent the two covenants God made with David, at the conception of the plan to build the House of God. One covenant was with David and the other covenant with the people of his kingdom.

Since the Hebrew meaning of the name "Jachin" can be translated "He shall establish," it must refer to the Covenant God made with David, to establish David's throne "forever." (II Sam. 7:16) The Hebrew meaning of the name "Boaz" is given as "In it is strength." It, in turn, must refer to the Covenant God made with the people, to "plant" them in "a place" of safety and in this covenant we find a promise of national strength. (II Sam 7:10)

THE HOLY PLACE

"And he built the walls of the house within with boards of cedar, both the floor of the house, and the walls of the ceiling: and he covered them on the inside with wood, and covered the floor of the house with planks of fir.

And he built twenty cubits on the sides of the house, both the floor and the walls with boards of cedar: he even built them for it within, even for the oracle, even for the most holy place.

And the house, that is, the temple before it, was forty cubits long.

And the cedar of the house with in, carved with knops and open flowers: all was cedar; there was no stone seen." (I Kings 6:15-18)

The Holy Place was a spacious room, given by some scholars as 60 feet long, 30 feet wide and 45 feet high. The interior walls were covered with panels of cedar wood carvings, overlaid with gold. The carvings consisted of cherubims, palm trees and flowers. The palm trees were considered the "tree of life" because they lived so long and bore so much fruit. The carvings described as *"knops and open flowers"* were the egg-shaped gourds and rosettes, so commonplace, as decorative motifs, in Solomon's time.

We may suppose that while the figures were in bas-relief, their outline was sunken, so that the upper surface did not extend beyond the surface of the boards. This is the most common form of engraving on the Egyptian monuments. Some idea of these designs may be gleaned from numerous fragments of carved ivory miniatures that have been recovered in quantity from Assyrian royal palaces in Iraq. One typical example from Numrud is shown below. Showing *"knops and open flowers."*

Phoenicians, from Tyre and Gebal (Byblos), were given the task of finishing the interiors and it seems that exact repetition of design was a favorite technique of the carvers.

The Biblical text refers to the panels as having been "overlaid" with gold, but students of Hebrew suggest the word "overlaid" is more accurately translated "inlaid." The floor was not then, "overlaid" with gold, but highlighted by skillful use of gold inlay.

The "windows of narrow lights" of I Kings 6:4 are now recognized as a "lattice type," or "windows with recessed frames," as indicated from a contemporary ivory inlay from Khorsabad.

The roof was made of beams and boards of cedar. Whether it was flat or gabled is not stated, but in keeping with the custom of the period, the former is more likely.

The floor was of cypress wood, and, like the walls and ceiling was "overlaid" with gold. Biblical "cypress" or "fir," was Cilician cypress, (Cypressus sempervirens) a very hard wood used today in the fine filigree wood carvings produced by the world famous carvers of Damascus. The fir, we know today, is too soft a wood and would have been unsuited for sustained wear.

The Howland-Garber reconstruction of Solomon's Temple also suggests the use of a kind of prefabrication; a method called "pallet" construction. A pallet is, in this sense, a large, self-supporting piece so constructed that it may be covered with boards and used as a floor, ceiling or wall panel.

These could have been fabricated outside the Temple area, carried into the structure and put in place silently. This would be in keeping with I Kings 6:7 that states the House was erected without the sound of a hammer, or any other tool of iron, being heard during the period of construction.

Nails could have been used in fastening together the pallets as evidenced by the discovery, at Ezion-Geber, of copper spikes produced at Solomon's refineries near the Red Sea. Fabricated cedar beams nailed together like I-beams would have provided support for the ceiling.

In the Holy Place were kept some relics from the Tabernacle: an Altar of Burnt Incense, now gold plated, the Table of Shewbread, and ten 7 branched "lampstands," instead of the "one" which was in the Tabernacle.

THE CANDLESTICKS

"And the candlesticks of pure gold, five on the right side, and five on the left, before the oracle, with the flowers, and the lamps, and the tongs of gold." (I Kings 7:49)

Lamps were used in Solomon's Temple to provide additional light for the priests doing their assigned tasks. The candlesticks of which the King James Version speaks (in connection with the Temple) are more accurately understood when considered as being lampholders. Candles were not used until after the Biblical period.

In earliest times a lamp consisted of a clay saucer filled with oil, on the rim of which rested a wick of twisted thread. About 2000 B.C. the first real lamps appeared. These early models were shaped like saucers and had their rims pinched, in four places, to form lips for holding the wicks.

From the Middle Bronze Age (2000-1500 B.C.) onward, the lamps had a single pinched lip becoming increasingly pinched. During the Israelite period lamps acquired bases and were found to have rims, pinched in seven places, for holding seven wicks.

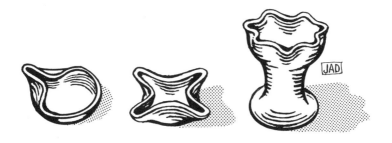

A metal stand with a tripod, found at Megiddo, together with a copper lamp unearthed at Ezion Geber (having seven wick channels) have served as guides in reconstructing the lamps of the Temple. It is doubtful if the "menorah" form of the lampstand, used in the Tabernacle and again in Herod's period, was used in Solomon's Temple, as an example from the period of the Israelite monarchy is yet to be found.

Such a seven-lipped lamp is described in Zech. 4:2 as *"a candlestick all of gold, with a bowl upon the top of it, and his seven lamps thereon, and seven pipes to the seven lamps, which are upon the tip thereof."*

In symbolism the seven lamps were supposed, by some scholars, to refer to the seven days of the week and by others to represent the seven planets. The planets were regarded as the "eyes" of God, which beheld everything.

The single, seven branched candelabra of the Holy Place in the Tabernacle, was replaced with 10 in Solomon's Temple. Five were on the right side and five on the left side. In a similar allegory, paralleling the 10 Lavers, we see revealed by the 10 candlesticks the foreknow - ledge that in the Christian era, light would be diffused by the 10 tribed House of Israel.

When the second temple was built by Jerubbabel, the 10 tribes were in exile so only one candlestick is found in his temple. It represented the tribe of Benjamin which was given as a light unto the House of Judah (I Kings 11:36) and was the only other tribe returning, with the remnant of Judah, from the Babylonian captivity.

The lamp, when taken together with "light" and "lampstand" had considerable symbolical power in the Biblical period. Light, emitted from a lamp, symbolizes universally, life as opposed to death, the realm of darkness.

Light and hence "lamp" also stands for the divine presence. *"I am the light of the world: he that followeth me shall not walk in darkness, but shall have the light of life;"* (John 8:12) *"the Lamb is the light thereof;"* (Rev. 21:23) *"In him was life: and the life was the light of men. And the light shineth in darkness; and the darkness comprehended it not."* (John 1:4,5)

Indeed, the light of the Holy Place went unheeded by many priests of the Old Covenant order, who labored in gross darkness, neglecting the great truths prefigured in the light of the candlesticks.

Today, we too, labor in darkness who fail to recognize the seven-branched lamp as typifying the Christian ministry, portrayed in the parallelism that exists between the Gospel of St. John and the Tabernacle services, reiterated in Solomon's Temple.

THE TABLE OF SHEWBREAD

"And Solomon made all the vessels that pertained unto the house of the Lord: the Altar of gold, and the table of gold, whereupon the shewbread was." (I Kings 7:48)

The Table of Shewbread, two cubits long, one cubit wide, and a cubit and a half high, held the twelve loaves of bread known as the "Bread of the Presence" which the priests brought, fresh, into the Holy Place each Sabbath. This offering was required to be continually in the presence of the Lord. (Exod. 25:30)

Presumably, the bread was unleavened although we have no Biblical confirmation of this matter. Josephus states that it was unleavened and the loaves, which were baked the day before the Sabbath, were brought into the Temple the morning of the Sabbath and heaped in two rows of six, one loaf leaning against another. A supply of pure frankincense, which was also placed on the table, was changed as a part of this ceremony. (Antiq. III 6:6; 10:7)

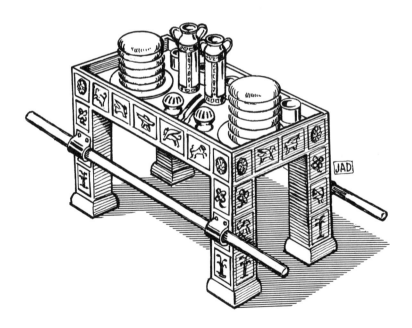

The twelve loaves represented the twelve tribes of Israel, who were to be, in a mystical sense, like our Lord, the "Bread of Life." (John 6:35) In the parable of the wheatfield, these mystical loaves were to be of the good seed, of the Kingdom, appointed for the nourishing of mankind.

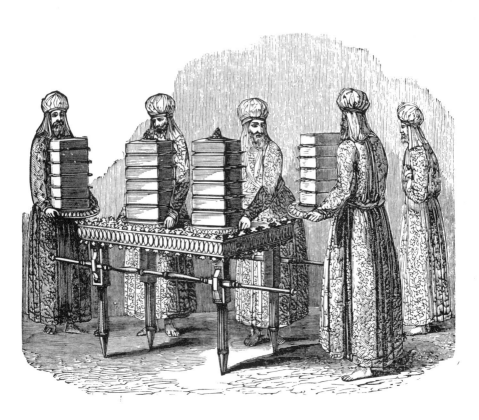

NINETEENTH CENTURY ENGRAVINGS OF THE TABLE OF SHEWBREAD
(UPPER) PRIESTS REPLACING OLD SHEWBREAD WITH NEW

Luke suggests that bread refers to the messianic banquet when he says, *"Blessed is he that shall eat bread in the kingdom of God."* (Luke 14:15)   The Christian proclaims the Lord's death, until He returns, whenever he partakes of the bread and the wine.

Jesus refers to Himself as the, *"true bread from heaven."* (John 6: 31-33)   This claim is strengthened in verse 35; *"I am the bread of life: he that cometh to me shall never hunger; and he that believeth on me shall never thirst."*

Upon the Table of Shewbread there stood other vessels (II Chron. 29:18) which would explain how the drink-offering of wine was handled in the Holy Place. (Exod. 29:40; Lev. 23:13,18,37)

The Shewbread and the Wine stood on the Table to typify the mystical body and blood of Christ, so offered by our Lord, at the Last Supper.   Each Sabbath, the priests partook of the sacrament when they ate the old loaves, after they had been replaced by new, (Lev. 24:5-9) and drank the drink-offering of wine.

Bread is often used in metaphorical expressions, both in the Old Testament and the New.   Except for the "breaking of bread," involved in the "Lord's Supper," it is used only allegorically, in reference to the coming kingdom of God or to Jesus Christ, Himself.   Bread and wine is what Melchizedek brought to Abraham (Gen 14:18) and Christ was *"made an high priest, forever, after the order of Melchisedec."* (Heb. 6:20)

The various "vessels" are not described in detail in the Scriptures which refers to *"the dishes thereof, and spoons thereof, and covers thereof, and bowls thereof, to cover withal: of pure gold shalt thou make them."* (Exod. 25:29; Num. 4:7)

"Covers" and "bowls" are sometimes translated as "flagons" and "chalices."   Josephus suggests that two golden cups, filled with frankincense, were set on the Table of Shewbread with the bread.

Although I Kings speaks of *"the table of gold, whereupon the shewbread was,"* II Chronicles cites *"the tables whereon the shewbread was set."* (II Chron. 4:19) And in an earlier verse (vs 8) says there were ten such tables, and that they were set in the Temple, *"five on the right side and five on the left."* There is no real contradiction here between Kings and Chronicles as different tables could have been used on different Sabbaths.   I Chronicles 28:16 refers to other tables and describes some of them being made of silver.

49

SUPPOSED FURNISHINGS AND VESSELS OF THE TABERNACLE BROUGHT INTO SOLOMON'S TEMPLE (EXCEPT MENORAH)

THE ALTAR OF BURNT INCENSE

"And Solomon made all the vessels that were for the house of God, the golden altar also..." (II Chron. 4:19)

I Kings refers to the Altar of Burnt Incense as the "Altar of Gold." It is not clear whether this item, as well as the Table of Shewbread was made new or were the original ones used in the Tent Tabernacle. If they were taken from the Tabernacle as is most likely the case, (II Chron. 5:5 Moffatt) then they may have been refinished with gold before being placed in the Temple.

A limestone altar, with horns, found by the Oriental Institute at Megiddo (circa twelfth century B.C.) has given us a reasonable likeness of the Altar. It was noted the dimensions were almost identical with those given in I Kings.

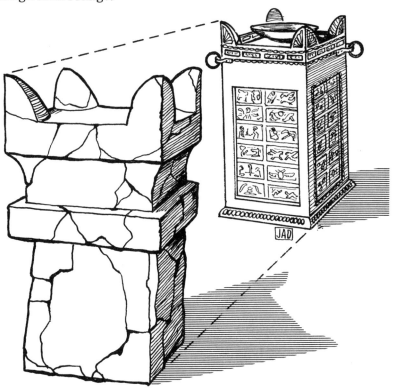

The addition of a small copper pan, placed between the horns, was in keeping with archaeological evidence of the use of such a device to guard against damage, from the heat, to the wood and the gold overlay of the top.

The offering of incense is treated as a very sacred rite wherever mentioned in the Old Testament. It was a capital offense for anyone, other than the High Priest, to make or offer this incense.

NINETEENTH CENTURY ENGRAVING OF THE ALTAR OF INCENSE

The incense, a compound of gums and spices, when burnt, emitted a "sweet smell" that the priests thought God, like His people, would enjoy. This was a continuance of God's instruction to Aaron. (Lev. 16:12,13) It was further believed that incense was effective in making atonement before Him . (Num 16:46-48)

A GOLDEN CENSER

FRANKINCENSE

While Zacharias was officiating at the Golden Altar, *"the whole multitude of the people were praying without, at the time of incense"* (Luke 1:10) thus revealing, in their act, the meaning of the ritual at the very time of its enactment.

In Rev. we read *"And another angel came and stood at the altar, having a golden censer; and there was given unto him much incense, that he should offer it with the prayers of all saints upon the golden altar which was before the throne. And the smoke of the incense, which came with the prayers of the saints, ascended up before God out of the angel's hand."* (Rev. 8:3,4)

HIGH PRIEST WITH GOLDEN CENSER

An interesting parallel between the offering of incense and prayer can be found in Ps. 141:2, Luke 1:10 and Rev. 8:3. The fragrance of the incense was symbolic of the prayers of the faithful, which when produced by the fire of the Holy Spirit acting upon thought, word, and deed, bound together in adoration, ascend acceptably unto God: *"Let my prayer be set forth before thee as incense; and the lifting up of my hands as the evening sacrifice."* *(Ps 141:2)*

SUPPOSED DRESS OF THE HIGH PRIEST AND LEVITE PRIEST

THE DOORS OF THE SANCTUARY

"And for the entering of the oracle he made doors of olive tree: the lintel and side posts were a fifth part of the wall.

The two doors also were of olive tree; and he carved upon them carvings of cherubims and palm trees and open flowers, and overlaid them with gold, and spread gold upon the cherubims, and upon the palm trees." (I Kings 6:31,32)

In keeping with the temple designs of the period, it is believed that the Inner Sanctuary had a floor elevated above the rest of the Temple. If so, steps would have been required ascending from the Holy Place to the entrance of the Inner Sanctuary or "Holy of Holies." In any case, a pair of folding olive wood doors separated the Oracle, or Ark, from the Holy Place.

The obscure phrase, "side posts were a fifth part," (Authorized Version) suggests there was something about the entrance to the Holy of Holies that was "pentagonal" or "fivefold." One interpretation is that the door posts were pentagonal, in cross section, thus allowing the doors to swing wider than a 90 degree angle.

The Moffatt translation, however provides grounds for a more logical hypothesis. *"He made doors of olive wood for the vestibule of the inner shrine; the vestibule and the pilasters formed a pentagon."* (I Kings 6:31 Moffatt) This would indicate a "vestibule" corresponding with the Temple "vestibule" or Porch, which was an architectural feature often found in temples of the East. If so, it would have been raised to the floor level of the Oracle.

The "pilasters" could refer to the "Almug wood pillars" mentioned in I Kings 10:12 for which no structural use has been determined. Extending to the ceiling of the Holy Place, these pentagon shaped sandalwood pillars, standing at each intersecting corner of the pentagonal "vestibule," focused the eyes of the observer, already cast upward by the flight of stairs leading up to the Inner Sanctuary, ever higher; conveying the feeling of "exaltation" expressed in the lofty doors and ceiling of the Temple.

The Septuagint Bible further suggests a porch before the Holy of Holies. *"And for the door way of the oracle he made doors of juniper wood, there were porches in a four-fold way."* (I Kings 6:31) "Four-fold way" would describe the four sides of the pentagon jutting out from the fifth side.(abutting to and paralleling the wall between the Holy Place and the Holy of Holies)

These doors were decorated with woodcarvings matching the wall panelling as were the fir doors to the Holy Place. Probably, the "Holy of Holies" doors were more elaborately carved and more richly "inlaid" with gold.

There is disagreement, among scholars, as to whether there was a veil in addition to the doors. The Book of Kings makes no mention of a veil, but in I Kings 6:21 we read, *"and he made a partition by the chains of gold across before the oracle."*

One interpretation gives "chains" as a design carved or incised upon the doors, while another supposes the passage originally read, *"and he drew the curtain, provided with golden chains, across before the oracle."* Josephus makes mention of a curtain before the doors and also, II Chron. 3:14 states there was a veil of *"blue, and purple, and crimson, and fine linen"* with figures of cherubim embroidered upon it. Notwithstanding, most scholars believe the veil may have been added, later, and was not a part of the Temple's original furnishings.

In the doors of the Sanctuary, a metonymy in wood may be discerned in the fact that the doorposts, lintels and the doors of the "Holy of Holies" were made of olive wood. Olive wood was the symbol of priestly Israel and since Israel was called to be a *"kingdom of priests and an holy nation"* (Exodus 19:6) and had become so, in the early years of the Christian dispensation; (I Peter 2:9) it follows that olive wood stands for the 12 tribes of Israel, in their ultimate condition of consecration.

As entrance to the "Holy of Holies" could only be effected through its doorway which was of olive wood, it shows entry into the true Temple must be, as it were, through the doorway of sanctified Israel as described in I Peter 2:9, *"a chosen generation, a royal priesthood, an holy nation, a peculiar people."*

In the Tabernacle there was no use of olive wood, the symbol of priestly Israel, but the use of oil of olives for lighting the Holy Place and for the annointing, was symbolic of Israel's priesthood.

THE HOLY OF HOLIES

"And the oracle he prepared in the house within, to set there the ark of the covenant of the Lord.

And the oracle in the forepart was twenty cubits in length, and twenty cubits in breadth and twenty cubits in height thereof: and he overlaid it with pure gold: and so covered the altar which was of cedar!" (I Kings 6:19,20)

The "Holy of Holies" was the inner Sanctuary, "the Most Holy Place," the receptacle for the Ark of the Covenant. It was in the shape of a perfect cube, estimated to be 30 feet square. (using 18" to a cubit)

In a cube we see something of transcendental perfection indicated: the length and breadth and height being equal. This significance of the cube is seen in the fact that the Holy of Holies, both, in the Wilderness Tabernacle and in Solomon's Temple were cubes. John the Revelator, describes the future "New Jerusalem" as a cube. (Rev. 21:16)

Since the Temple, on a whole, is given as 30 cubits in height, (45 feet) there is a difference of 10 cubits, or 15 feet, to explain. The accepted explanation is that in addition to the floor being raised, the ceiling was lowered, the area below the floor added to the space above equalling the 10 cubits.

There is no Biblical conflict with this hypothesis although nothing is said about a difference in height, anywhere in the Scriptures. Archaeological analogies, ranging from early Assyrian temples to Phoenician temples of Solomon's period, justify raising the floor of the inner Sanctuary.

The space resulting between the ceiling of the Holy of Holies and the ceiling of the Temple proper is often mentioned, by writers on Solomon's Temple, as an "upper" or "secret" chamber, quoting I Chron. 28:11, and II Chron. 3:9, where certain "upper chambers" are mentioned. It is more likely that these referred to a part of the upper tier of the Side Chambers.

As in the case of the Holy Place, the interior of the Inner Sanctuary was covered with carved panels of cedar "overlaid" with gold, probably more richly ornamented. There were no windows. The only light came from the Holy Place with its "lattice" windows and lampstands.

Although the devout could gaze from the courtyard through the opened doors, and the priests could look, from the Holy Place, into the darkened chamber; only the High Priests saw its esoteric beauty, from the inside. In like manner, just as many had seen Jesus, only His disciples could really say, *"We beheld His glory, the glory as of the only begotten of the Father, full of grace and truth."* (John 1:14)

The Holy of Holies, was, typically, the place of His "throne," (Ezek. 43:7) seen only by the High Priest during the Day of Atonement. This Day of Atonement was the one day in the whole year when the High Priest entered into the Holy of Holies where the Ark of the Covenant and the Cherubim were over the Mercy Seat. Divested of his robes *"for glory and for beauty,"* he was clad only in pure white linen. Alone, lonely, without outward beauty (*"no beauty that we should desire him"*) except that of symbolical purity, the High Priest went in once a year to offer for his own sins and those of the people.

Then came a ceremony unique and significant in character. It was the ceremony of the "Scapegoat." (Azazel) The origin of the ceremony began with the Tabernacle in the Wilderness and is given in Leviticus chapter 16. Two goats were chosen and brought to the door of the Tabernacle. Lots were cast, one "for the Lord" and one for the "Scapegoat." The one on whom the lot *"for the Lord"* fell was offered as a sin-offering and its blood taken into the Holy of Holies as an atonement. The "Scapegoat," was to be presented alive before the

Lord *"to made an atonement with him, and to let him go for a scape-goat into the wilderness."*

THE SCAPEGOAT SENT INTO THE WILDERNESS — FROM AN ENGRAVING

But before that was done, the High Priest had to lay both hands on the head of the live goat and confess all the iniquities of the Children of Israel, *"all their transgressions in all of their sins, putting them upon the head of the goat"* and then *"shall send him away by the hand of a fit man into the wilderness."* (v. 21) *"And the goat shall bear upon him all their iniquities unto a land not inhabited: and he shall let go the goat in the wilderness."* (v. 22)

Thus atonement was accomplished by the offering of blood and sprinkling it before the Mercy Seat. The live goat was public manifestation and proof of acceptance of the sacrifice in the Divine Presence and the transference of guilt from the sinner to the Scapegoat. What was accomplished "within" was manifested "without." It signified the dismissal, (Azazel — dismissal, R.V. margin) of our sins. Christ is our "Azazel," our "Scapegoat," *"cut off out of the land of the living: for the transgression of my people was he stricken."* (Isa. 53:8)

The Book of Hebrews confirms the inner Sanctuary as symbolic of the redemption wrought by Christ, *"having therefore brethren, boldness to enter into the holiest by the blood of Jesus."* (Heb. 10:19) In yet another sense, the Holy of Holies was a copy or "shadow" (Heb. 8:5) of "heaven." (Heb. 9:24)

THE GUARDIAN CHERUBIM

"And within the oracle he made two cherubim of olive tree, each ten cubits high.

And five cubits was the one wing of the cherub, and five cubits the other wing of the cherub: from the uttermost part of the one wing unto the uttermost part of the other were ten cubits.

And the other cherub was ten cubits: both the cherubims were of one measure and one size.

The height of the one cherub was ten cubits, and so was it of the other cherub.

And he set the cherubims within the inner house: and they stretched forth the wings of the cherubims, so that the wing of the one touched the one wall, and the wing of the other touched the other wall; and their wings touched one another in the midst of the house.

And he overlaid the cherubims with gold." (I Kings 6:23-28)

One of the most difficult Biblical objects to illustrate is the Cherubim mentioned in connection with Solomon's Temple. Having no precise description of them, other than they represented certain "living creatures," (Ezek. 1:5) artistic concepts have consequently produced a wide variety of impressions. Time was when "cherubim" were represented as being plump, winged infants or young females.

Today, influenced by the unique, "visionary" descriptions of the cherubim, found in the Book of Ezekiel, many Bible scholars have conceived them to be "hybred" creatures: part bird, part animal and part man.

Most attempts to reconstruct them, however, fail to accurately take into account Ezeliel's description of a cherubim, but are influenced rather by statues and portraits of the Assyrian winged bull or lion and the Egyptian winged sphinx. This has generally resulted in the cherubim being portrayed as a winged lion with a man's head.

It is debatable whether such interpretations are helpful, even as suggestions, where they fail to be supported by whatever Scriptural evidence we have. An inexpert viewer is likely to get a very wrong impression.

For this reason no illustrations will be presented, herein, of the two Guardian Cherubim that were placed in the Holy of Holies of Solomon's Temple.

Ezekiel saw in his vision, the Cherubim in a state of mystic anima-

61

tion and unity, which could not be realized in a static model, but which was nevertheless an intended portrayal of historical action.

"And every one had four faces, and every one had four wings.

And their feet were straight feet; and the sole of their feet was like the sole of a calf's foot: and they sparkled like the colour of burnished brass. And they had the hands of a man under their wings on their four sides; and they four had their faces and their wings.

Their wings were joined one to another; they turned not when they went; they went every one straight forward.

As for the likeness of their faces, they four had the face of a man, and the face of a lion, on the right side: and they four had the face of an ox on the left side; they four also had the face of an eagle." (Ezekiel 1:6-10)

It can be shown that Ezekiel's description of the four "cherubim" are symbolic of each of the four "brigades" of Israel, in the four-square Wilderness Camp. The four cherubim are described as each having four faces: lion, ox, man and eagle. These are found to be the emblems of the leading tribes. (Judah, Ephraim, Reuben and Dan)

Ezekiel further states the "four creatures" came out of the "north." (Ezek. 1:4) Since each face of the "man" is represented as seen in a front position and coming from the "north," the face (lion) on the right would be placed in the "east," the face (ox) on the left in the west, and the face (eagle) in the rear or the north.

These positions correspond perfectly with the positions assigned to the tribes of Judah, Ephraim, Reuben and Dan, in the Wilderness Camp.

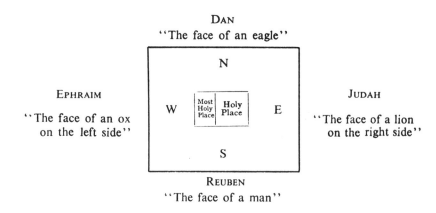

DAN
"The face of an eagle"

EPHRAIM

"The face of an ox
on the left side"

JUDAH

"The face of a lion
on the right side"

REUBEN
"The face of a man"

62

THE ARK OF THE COVENANT

"And they shall make an ark of shittim wood: two cubits and a half shall be the length thereof, and a cubit and a half the breadth thereof, and a cubit and a half the height thereof.

And thou shall overlay it with pure gold, within and without shalt thou overlay it, and shalt make upon it a crown of gold round about.

And thou shalt make two cherubims of gold, of beaten work shalt thou make them, in the two ends of the mercy seat." (Exod. 25:10,11,18)

The Ark of the Covenant was a small wooden box approximately 45" by 27" by 27" overlaid with gold. It had a dished lid and golden rings, one at each of its four corners, for two porter poles. It was originally the one made of acacia wood (Exod. 25:10) by Moses. The extended descriptions of the Ark are found in Exodus 25: vs. 10 to 22.

During the wilderness years of wandering, the porter poles were never removed from the Ark, whereas they were removed from all other furniture, when the camp rested. This symbolically indicated that any resting place of the Ark, during the forty years in the wilderness, was but temporary, until its destination was reached.

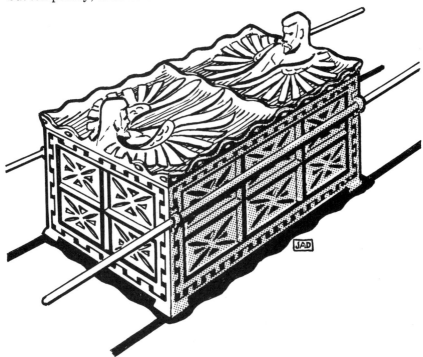

The two "cherubims" placed on top of the Ark, in keeping with the "cherubim" described by Ezekiel, symbolized all Israel, in perpetual remembrance, before the Throne of God.

The lid of the Ark, known as the "Mercy Seat," was made of "pure gold" and was annually sprinkled with the blood of a goat and of a bullock according to Lev. 16:14, 15. The interpretation of this act of the High Priest, can be found in the New Testament, in Heb. 9:vv. 11 and 12. *"But Christ, being come an high priest of good things to come, by a greater and more perfect tabernacle, not made with hands, that is to say, not of this building, neither by the blood of goats and calves, but by his own blood he entered in once into the Holy Place, having obtained eternal redemption for us."*

Thus by employing symbols for the persons who were the nearest and furthest from God — Priests by the bullocks and heathens by the goats — the Temple ritual foreshadowed that, on behalf of all mankind, Christ entered once and for all time into the presence of the Throne of God, to effect our atonement. (Matt. 25:32-34)

The Ark was the symbolical seat of Yahveh's authority in the "Most Holy Place." The Manna and Aaron's rod deposited therein, during the period of the Wilderness Tabernacle, depicted the true "Bread of Life" who would come down from Heaven; the true "High Priest." Through the foreknowledge that this symbolism would be fulfilled in Jesus Christ, in the True Tabernacle, those items were therefore not continued in the Temple of Solomon, which was a type of the Post-Resurrection Christian Era. (I Kings 8:9)

So, accordingly, there rested in the typical Temple only the Tablets of the Law, the typology of which has not yet been terminated by reason of fulfillment. For Christ says in Matt. 5:17,18, *"think not that I am come to destroy the law or the prophets, I am not come to destroy, but to fulfill. For verily I say unto you, till heaven and earth pass, one jot or one tittle shall in no way pass from the law, till all be fulfilled."*

The Law was not made void by Christianity. (Rom. 3:31) It is written, in Romans, that we are not *under* the law but under "grace" (Rom. 6:15) but, the 23rd verse adds: *"For the wages of sin is death, but the gift of God is eternal life through Jesus Christ our Lord."* Since "death" has not been destroyed (I Cor. 15:25,26) it follows that "under grace" simply means that we are free from the condemnation or "curse" of the law. (Gal. 3:13)

THE SIDE CHAMBERS

"And against the wall of the house he built chambers round about, against the walls of the house round about, both of the temple and of the oracle: and he made chambers round about:

The nethermost chamber was five cubits broad, and the middle was six cubits broad, and the third was seven cubits broad: for without in the walls of the house he made narrowed rests round about, that the beams should not be fastened in the walls of the house.

The door for the middle chamber was in the right side of the house: and they went up with winding stairs into the middle chamber, and out of the middle into the third. " (I Kings 6:5,6,8)

The side chambers built all around the outside of the building, except the Porch were arranged in three stories: the first 5 cubits broad, the second 6 cubits broad and the third 7 cubits broad, each being 5 cubits high.

Offsets in the main walls were made to accommodate supporting beams, so they need not be inserted into the main walls, and the result was the increasing width of the stories.

Insufficient details are given in the Scriptures to fully understand the exact design or purpose of the rooms. Ezekiel, in translation, leaves the impression that there were thirty-three cubicles on each of the three floors; ninety-nine cubicles in all.

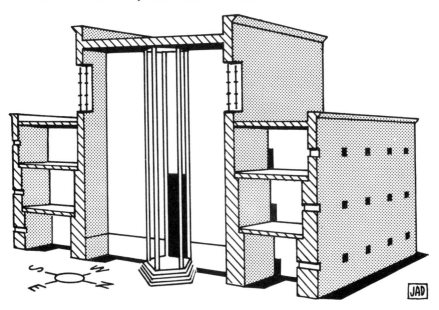

The entrance to the side chambers was on the "right side" of the building, which could mean either the north or the south side, depending on where the observer was standing. No windows are indicated in descriptions of the side chambers and whether the door opened from the inside or outside is a matter of debate. Access only from the interior main room has been suggested from their use as "treasure chambers" or "storage vaults" for priestly garments and equipment. In any case, I Kings 6:8 speaks of a door in the "right side of the house." This would indicate an exterior opening and would be logical, as a means of bringing supplies into the Temple "storage rooms" without profaning the Holy Place.

From the lowest floor of the side chambers there were "winding stairs" into the second level and out of the second into the third. Various efforts to translate the Hebrew phrase "winding stairs" have been made, but the precise meaning is still not clear. It refers to some means of getting from one story to the other.

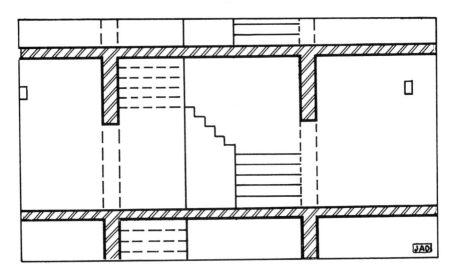

Modern translations have given different interpretations for the King James words "winding stairs" "trap door" in Moffatt, "a circular trap door" in the Amer. Trans., and simply "stairs" in the RSV. Reconstructions naturally vary widely in this detail.

THE ALTAR OF BURNT OFFERINGS

"Moreover he made an altar of brass, twenty cubits the length thereof, and twenty cubits the breadth thereof, and ten cubits the height thereof" (II Chron. 4:1).

In the court outside the Temple and on the right side stood the Altar of Burnt Offerings. A lack of archaeological evidence makes it impossible to reconstruct, with certainty, the exact details of design and decorations of the Altar. However, the most acceptable, authoritative interpretation is that the sides were straight and a flight of stairs led up to the top upon which sat a large metal grate, standing on low feet.

Using the length of the common cubit (approx. 18") the size of the Altar was about 30 feet square, at the base, and about 15 feet high. No dimensions are given for the width of the steps or their number. It can be assumed they were of sufficient width for two persons to pass. The steps faced east, as did the Temple.

I Kings 1:50 indicates the Altar had horns. A number of stone altars, with horns in the corners, have been found in excavations at Megiddo and other places in Palestine. These were of Solomon's period and would suggest the Temple Altar also had horns, in the corners, and was of hewn stone. I Kings 9:25 designates the Altar as one which Solomon had built. Evidently it had not been assigned to Hiram's metal artisans to construct. This would, again, suggest the basic Altar was of stone.

The term "brass" in II Chron. 4:1 and "brasen" in I Kings 8:64 and II Kings 16:15 would seem to indicate a top portion of bronze or that the Altar was covered with bronze plates, a technique supported by archaeological evidence.

Another form for the Altar is suggested by the visionary Altar, of the future, found in Ezek. 43:13-17 which describes a three-stage structure, each stage smaller than the one below; like a Babylonian Ziggurat or tower — Temple. A more recent, modern, reconstruction model of the Altar (based on Ezekiel's description) has resulted in a "controversial" step-stage tower. The steps, in the form of riser-ramps, encircle the Altar as they rise steadily to the top platform.

On the blaze atop the Altar, the priest put parts of the sacrificial animals. These sacrifices, of the individual and of the nation, in themselves did not cover sin; they were a prophetic allegory to the one "sacrifice acceptable" (Phil. 4:18) whereby sin itself is covered. *"Christ was once offered to bear the sins of many"* (Heb. 9:28);

"For he hath made him to be sin for us, who knew no sin; that we might be made the righteousness of God in him;" (II Cor. 5:21) *"God sending his own Son in the likeness of sinful flesh, and for sin, condemned sin in the flesh."* (Rom. 8:3)

The killing of the sacrificial animal was done near the Altar in order that the blood could be collected and sprinkled on the horns of the Altar. (Lev. 1:5) The shedding of blood, according to law, must be performed *"on the side of the altar northward before the Lord."* (Lev. 1:11) It is assumed this would be continued in Solomon's Temple, thus prophetically foreshadowing the very direction of the coming Sacrifice, in the age of the True Tabernacle — the Christian era. For Jesus Christ was crucified north of the city near Golgotha (the place of the skull) which is still recognized by its spectacular rock formation, the caves in the rock, suggestive of eyeless sockets in a skull.

THE MOLTEN SEA

"And he made a molten sea, ten cubits from the one brim to the other: it was round all about, and his height was five cubits: and a line of thirty cubits did compass it round about.

And under the brim of it round about there were knops compassing it, ten in a cubit, compassing the sea round about: the knops were cast in two rows, when it was cast.

It stood upon twelve oxen, three looking toward the north, and three looking toward the west, and three looking toward the south, and three looking toward the east: and the sea was set above upon them, and all their hinder parts were inward.

And it was an handbreadth thick, and the brim thereof was wrought like the brim of a cup, with flowers of lilies: it contained two thousand baths." (I Kings 7:23-25)

In the court yard just left of the entrance to the Temple was the great brass bowl cast by Hiram of Tyre, the widow's son (I Kings 7: 13,14). The bronze used in the casting was that taken, as spoil, by King David in his wars. (I Chron. 18:8)

I Kings describes the Sea as round, 10 cubits (15 feet) in diameter and 5 cubits (7½ feet) high. The circumference is given as 30 cubits. Since the exact circumference holds the relationship to it diameter of 3.14159 to 1, the discrepancy noted is an example of how the Bible often avoids fractions in favor of round numbers.

The bronze (cast copper alloy) bowl was about 3 inches thick and its brim was turned outward like a lily or lotus flower and gave the appearance of a cup. Under the brim were two rows of ornamental gourds ("knops") which seemingly were cast with the vessel.

It is not precisely known which flower represented the "lily," but various species of "Gladiolus" or the Iris" are favoured. The lily is often used in the Scriptures in an allegorical sense; Hosea likens the lily to Israel, *"I will be as the dew unto Israel: he shall grow as the lily, and cast forth his roots as Lebanon* (the House of David)."(Hosea 14:5) Solomon further confirms this allegory, *"As the lily among thorns, so is my love among the daughters."* (Song. 2:2)

According to I Kings the Sea held 2000 baths of water, estimate by some scholars to equal approximately 10,000 gallons of water. It is interesting to note that the capacity of the Sea, as given, is exactly 50 times that of the Coffer in the Kings Chamber of the Great Pyramid.

The great bowl rested upon twelve bronze oxen facing, at right angles, in four directions, each trio facing the major points of the compass. This may indicate the need of the priest to make daily washings, the year round through all the seasons of the year, to symbolize the essential daily cleansing of their spiritual selves.

Although the purposes for the Molten Sea are not given in Kings, it performed the same function as its predecessor, the Laver of the Tabernacle, but on a much larger scale. II Chron. 4:6 states that the "Molten Sea" was for the priests to wash in, while the "ten Lavers" were used for washing individual offerings.

It should be noted that the washing of the priests was not performed in the Temple, but outside, where in fitting allegory, all uncleanliness must be left behind before taking one's place in the True Temple.

The symbolism of the Sea probably had cosmic overtones, "Sea" representing the oceans (Gen. 1:9,10) and together with the Altar, symbolizing the mountains, on the other side of the court, proclaimed to worshippers that the God, who is worshipped here, is God of all the earth.

In the reign of King Ahaz, the Sea was taken off the bronze oxen and placed on a "pavement of stones" (II Kings 16:17) and finally, it was broken up by the Chaldeans and carried to Babylonia.

THE LAVERS

"And he made ten bases of brass; four cubits was the length of one base, and four cubits the breadth thereof, and three cubits the height of it.

Then made he ten lavers of brass; one laver contained forty baths: and every laver was four cubits; and upon every one of the ten bases one laver.

And he put five bases on the right side of the house, and five on the left side:..." (I Kings 7:27,38,39)

Among the other bronze objects made by Hiram of Tyre were the 10 "brass" stands on wheels with "brass" bowls of water upon them. (I Kings 7:27-37)   The stands or "bases" (trolleys — Moffatt trans.) were covered with carved panels, depicting lions, oxen and cheribum, framed in decorative borders.   Each base had four bronze chariot (six-spoked) wheels which turned on axels made of "one piece with the trolley." (Moffatt - I Kings 7:32)

The Lavers of brass each held 40 "baths" of water. (I Kings 7:38) A "bath" is estimated, by various scholars, to be from 4½ to 5½ American gallons. Using an estimate of 5 gallons to a bath, each Laver would hold around 200 gallons of water.   According to II Chron. 4:6, this water was used to wash the individual sacrifices, for the burnt offering.

Although much detail is given in the Scriptures as to their design and purpose, most attempts to reconstruct the Lavers have produced models of impractical heights for their purpose.   The total height, in most cases, is well over the height of a man.

However, if we take the dimensions, as given in I Kings 7:27, which gives the Laver as 4 cubits (estimated 6 feet) square and 3 cubits (estimated 4½ feet) high as the overall size of the Laver, much of our problem is solved.   Just as the height of the wheels (a cubit and a half) is generally recognized as part of the total height, so could the "round compass (described in v. 35) of half a cubit high" (estimated 9 inches), on top of the base, be considered as part of the total height of the base.

Verse 31 of I Kings 7 (Moffatt) which is only describing the framework of the base, has often been used by scholars to picture a support or "crown" of 1½ cubits high on top of the base to support the Laver. This would erroneously increase the height to well over 6 feet.

Into the round compass (saucer — Moffatt) was placed the laver

(Bronze pot — Moffatt) having a rim diameter of 4 cubits, the same width as the base (6 feet). Assuming the laver nestled into the 9 inch saucer, the height of the laver above the saucer would be approximately 9 inches, making a total height of about 5¼ feet.

The 10 Lavers, in a prophetic sense, indicated the 10 tribed House of Israel through which, in a future dispensation, would flow the spiritual "water" for the cleansing of the offerings of mankind. The House of Israel was the nation referred to, in Matt. 21:43, when Jesus told the leaders of the House of Judah, *"the kingdom of God shall be taken from you and given to a nation bringing forth the fruits thereof."* ("...given to a people who will produce the fruits of it" — Amplified Bible)

"LIVELY STONES"

"Ye also as lively stones, are built up a spiritual house, a holy priesthood, to offer up spiritual sacrifices, acceptable to God by Jesus Christ." (I Peter 2:5)

In erecting Solomon's Temple, the great stones were brought, individually, from darkness into light; hewn, shaped and polished to form the local habitation of God.

The material Temple, built by King Solomon, symbolizes the Spiritual Temple of God. Each man is a "stone," dead in darkness, till lifted up by another. Through a progression of religious experiences, typified by being "hewn," "shaped" and "polished," symbolizing the work of regeneration, he improves his mind, uplifts his principles and refines his morals thereby becoming "acceptable." Then, filled with His Spirit, man becomes a part of the Spiritual Temple of God.

In allegory, each man is a master builder. As he builds his own body through which he must function, he is erecting a spiritual house. An invisible temple fashioned without the sound of hammer or the voices of workmen. This work must be done of our own free-will, yet it must be under the direction of the "Master Builder."

God gave the plans of Solomon's Temple to men, but men had to work out the plans given. Had not men worked as God planned, Solomon's Temple would never have been completed. God has given each of us the plan of the Spiritual Temple. The plan is His Word and the Bible (the plan in print) must regulate our every act. It should constantly remind us of the duties we owe to God, to our fellow men, and to ourselves.

To God, by never speaking His name but with the awe and reverence which is due to our Father, by imploring His aid in all lawful undertakings, and by looking to Him, in every emergency, for comfort and support.

To our fellow man, by acting with him fairly, justly, honorably; by relieving his distresses and soothing his afflictions.

To ourselves, by prudence and a well-regulated discipline conducive to pure and virtuous conduct, whereby we may be able to do what God demands of us; in order that we may be fitted to the place, we are to fill, in the Living Temple of God.

The doctrine of the Apostle Paul repeatedly affirms, in the New Testament, the existence of a mystical Christian Temple. *"Know ye not that ye are the temple of God...which temple ye are.*(I Cor. 3:16,17;

73

Eph. 2:22) An examination of the details given, concerning this now present mystical temple, shows its pattern is none other than that of Solomon's Temple.

The Bible speaks of yet another "stone." It is referred to by way of pre-eminence, as being a "head stone." Jesus, quoting from Psalms 118:22,23 said, *"Did ye never read in the Scriptures, The stone which the builders rejected, the same is become the head of the corner: this is the Lord's doing, and is marvellous in our eyes?* (Matt. 21:42) At that time, He was speaking of the rejection of Himself by the remnant of the House of Judah.

In the fourth chapter of the Book of Acts it is recorded: *"Then Peter, filled with the Holy Spirit, said unto them, Ye rulers of the people, and elders of Israel, if we this day be examined of the good deed done to the impotent man, by what means he is made whole: be it known unto you all, and to all the people of Israel, that by the name of Jesus of Nazareth, whom ye crucified, whom God raised from the dead, even by him doth this man stand here before you whole. This is the stone which was set at nought of you builders, which is become the head of the corner."* (Acts 4:8-11)

Again, Peter says, in his first epistle, the second chapter, seventh verse: *"Unto you therefore which believe he is precious; but unto them which be disobedient, the stone which the builders disallowed, the same is made the head of the corner."*

Although the Bible gives no account of a rejected stone, by the builders of Solomon's Temple, it is evident that Peter, as well as Jesus, made reference to a rejection, as a symbol of the rejection of Christ, by the House of Judah.

The early disciples so understood it to be, therefore the central theme of the Gospel is the "rejection" and "glorious resurrection" of Jesus Christ. Having shed His blood as the one acceptable sacrifice, redeeming His people Israel, He conquered death and thereby opened the way to eternal life; to all who would believe on His name.

He triumphantly entered, not into the Temple made with hands, but into heaven itself to constitute the foundation of the True Temple on which the salvation of mankind rests. He is the "Head Stone" which beautifies, strengthens and completes the Spiritual Temple of God.

DEDICATION OF THE TEMPLE

"Lift up your head, O ye gates; even lift them up, ye everlasting doors; and the King of glory shall come in.

Who is this King of glory? The Lord of hosts, he is the King of Glory, Selah." (Psalms 24:9,10)

Accounts of the opening of the Temple for daily use are given in I Kings 8:1-11, and II Chron. 5:1-14. From these authorities we learn that in the seventh month of the same year, as that in which "the house" was completed, it was formally dedicated. The gathering for this momentous occasion was a comparatively small one. Those who were officially assembled were representative men only. First were the twelve Princes of chiefs of the Tribes. To them were added the Elders of Israel, which according to Exod. 24:1 numbered seventy.

Doubtless many spectators were also present for the dedication, as the time was that of the Feast of Tabernacles. This was held on the fifteenth and seven following days of the first month of the civil war, being the seventh month (Tishri) of the ecclesiastical year.

The first act of dedication was to bring the Ark of the Covenant, which rested on Mount Ophel (having been brought from Kirjath-Jearim before Solomon's birth) "into the oracle of the house."(I Kings 8:1-11) Solomon himself led the procession, the national representatives following. Last came the priests blowing silver trumpets, and Levites, carrying the sacred burden of the Ark and all the holy vessels that had been in the tent on Ophel.

The distance to be traversed was less than half a mile. Music and singing of all kinds accompanied this ceremony and the priests stood dressed in pure white linen at the east end of the altar playing upon musical instruments. Trumpeters and singers thanked God, saying, *"For he is good; for his mercy endureth forever."* (II Chron. 5:13)

As of old, at every six paces, oxen and fatlings were sacrificed before the on-coming Ark. (II Sam. 6:13) The whole way was thus strewn with sacrificial blood, and the records agree in stating that the sheep and oxen sacrificed could not be told nor numbered for the multitude. (I Kings 8:5 and II Chron. 5:6)

The Priests received the Ark at the Temple door from the hands of the Levites and conveyed it to its place in the Oracle of the House. It was finally deposited by the High Priest in the Holy of Holies, at the western side, between the out-stretched wings of the Giant Cherubims. As the Priests retired from the Holy Place, the golden cloud of the Shekinah filled the Temple with the Glory of the Lord.

SOLOMON DEDICATES THE TEMPLE

Then Solomon stood before the altar of the Lord in the midst of the assembly and raised his hands to heaven in prayer. Solomon prayed to the Lord in deep humility and great thankfulness for the mercies shown His people. His words recalled the Lord's faithfulness in fulfilling His word, and, with prophetic insight, he envisioned the days to come when the people would pass through times of trouble and would need to experience anew the presence of their God leading them through captivity and judgment into a new age of peace and prosperity.

In his prayer, Solomon like David before him, fully recognized the extent of the power and majesty of the Lord *"But will God indeed dwell on the earth? Behold, the heaven and heaven of heavens cannot contain thee; how much less this house that I have builded?* (I Kings 8:27) This question can be answered in the affirmative. God will indeed dwell on the earth, in person and in visible form in all eternity, as He now dwells in heaven. (Isa 66:22-24; Titus 2:13; Rev. 21:1-27; 22:4,5) This does not mean, however, that His presence will be limited to the earth anymore than it is now limited to heaven.

In his plea before the Lord, Solomon referred to both individual and national shortcomings and called upon the Lord to forgive when His people became willing to conform with the requirements which would bring about the answer to their prayers: *"And Solomon stood before the altar of the Lord in the presence of all the congregation of Israel, and spread forth his hands toward heaven: And he said, Lord God of Israel, there is no God like thee, in the heaven above, or on earth beneath, who keepest covenant and mercy with thy servants that walk before thee with all their heart:...And hearken thou to the supplication of thy servant, and of thy people Israel, when they shall pray toward this place: and hear thou in heaven thy dwelling place: and when thou hearest, forgive."* (I Kings 8:22,30)

The Kings petition covered many aspects of the lives of the people; relationships between neighbors, times of war, weather conditions, famine, pestilence, crop failures and sickness. It is interesting to note the explicit instructions regarding the prayers of the people: The prayer for God's presence with His people, in time of national defeat, when they *"make supplication unto thee in this house;"* (I Kings 8:33,34) in times of famine or pestilence *"if they pray toward this place;"* (vv. 35-37) in war, if they *"shall pray unto the Lord toward the city which thou hast chosen, and toward the house that I have built for thy name."* (vv. 44,45)

As a point of interest, the floor plans of many great cathedrals and churches in Europe, Britain and America run east to west, with the altar in the "east." Thus many people today, in the "west," are unknowingly praying "east" toward the Temple site. Masonic Temple's are also designed, if possible, east to west. Although the altar is not placed in the "east," the fact that each Lodge is a symbol of the Temple would make any supplication therein symbolically "in this house."

The "east" is also traditionally associated with the Lord's return. Just as the wise men saw His star in the "east," so many Christians look for the sign of His second coming, in the "eastern sky." *"For as the lightning cometh out of the east, and shineth even unto the west; so shall also the coming of the Son of man be;"* (Matt. 24:27) *"And then shall appear the sign of the Son of Man in heaven."* (Matt. 24:30)

So effective was Solomon's supplication for God's mercy to rest at all times upon the people that fire came down from heaven to consume their sacrifices and the Glory of the Lord filled the Temple. (II Chron. 7:1) It is also written: *"And the Lord appeared to Solomon by night, and said unto him, I have heard thy prayer...If I shut heaven that there be no rain, or if I command the locust to devour the land, or if I send pestilence among my people; if my people, which are called by my name, shall humble themselves, and pray, and seek my face, and turn from their wicked ways; then will I hear from heaven, and will forgive their sins, and heal their land."* (II Chron. 7:12-14)

In the prayer Solomon offered at the dedication of the Temple an indication can be found that he recognized the concept implied by the replacement of the Wilderness Tabernacle with a permanent building. The Israelites called their Temple the *"House of the Lord,"* but thought of it only as a place where God's *name* dwelt. (I Kings 8:16,20; 9:3) Solomon seemed to sense the prophetic symbolism of the Temple when he asked, *"But will God indeed dwell on the earth?"* (I Kings 8:27)

In the age of the New Jerusalem, God no longer needs a Temple or Tabernacle through which to reveal His power and glory: *"And I John saw the holy city, new Jerusalem, coming down from God out of heaven, prepared as a bride adorned for her husband. And I heard a great voice out of heaven saying, Behold, the tabernacle of God is with men, and he will dwell with them, and they shall be his people, and God himself shall be with them, and be their God...And I saw no temple therein: for the Lord God Almighty and the Lamb are the temple of it."* (Rev. 21:2,3,22)

The very enactment of placing the Ark in the Holies of Holies, prophetically portrayed the glorious "Living Temple" in the coming "Kingdom of God on earth," as the "Lord of Hosts" takes His rightful place as "King of Glory."

"Howbeit the Lord would not destroy the house of David because of the covenant that he had made with David..." (II Chron. 21:7)

Perhaps one of the most important truths to be revealed by a study of Solomon's Temple is the fulfillment of the symbolism found in the two pillars, "Jachin" and "Boaz."

In II Sam. Chapter 7, we read where, in honor of David's noble thought, God would add to his (David's) regal house of cedar, yet another house, to bear his name, which would be both everlasting and of his own loins.

Nathan the Prophet tells David, in vv. 11-13, *"Also the Lord telleth thee that he will make thee an house. And when thy days be fulfilled, and thou shall sleep with thy fathers, I will set up thy seed after thee, which shall proceed out of thy bowels, and I will establish his kingdom. He shall build a house for my name, and I will establish the throne of his kingdom forever."*

Thus we see David's pious desire was reciprocated by God, and what David would build to Him, He also, in an allegorical sense, would build unto David, a house — a kingdom and a throne — forever in safety, but not in the Holy Land. This land had once been occupied by others, who now surrounded them as enemies.

God says in v. 10: *"Moreover, I will appoint a place for my people Israel, and will plant them, that they may dwell in a place of their own, and move no more, neither shall the children of wickedness afflict them any more, as beforetime."*

Two Covenants are implied here. One was symbolized by the pillar Jachin and related to the establishment of "David's House" or "Throne." The other was symbolized by the pillar Boaz and concerned the moving, of the people of the kingdom, to an "appointed" place.

Since they were then in Palestine, it follows that the "appointed" place had to be somewhere else, a new place, future to David's time.

However, the Throne and the inhabitants of the Kingdom remained in Palestine, for several centuries. During this time the two pillars stood, in front of Solomon's Temple, as a constant reminder of the two Covenants.

THE CORONATION THRONE

THE THRONE OF DAVID

"I have made a covenant with my chosen, I have sworn unto David my servant.

Thy seed will I establish for ever, and build up thy throne to all generations, Selah." (Psalm 89:3,4)

Here we have a Covenant and an Oath. David's seed is to be established, by God, "for ever;" not just for so many centuries, but in perpetuity. It was unconditional, even with the contingency of the seed forsaking the law and breaking the statutes; *"If his children forsake my law, and walk not in my judgments; if they break my statutes and keep not my commandments; Then will I visit their transgression with the rod, and their iniquity with stripes."* (Psalm 89:30-33)

In spite of disobedience to God, the Throne and the Royal Dynasty was not to cease. Peter, in his sermon on the day of Pentecost (Acts 2:29,30) referred to the immutability of this Covenant. Therefore, where is David's Throne today? This prophecy, of the enduring future of David's Throne, was uttered in the year 975 B.C. About 390 years later, the last king of David's line ceased to rule — so we are commonly told. If this were really true, then one great Covenant of the Bible — the Davidic Kingship Covenant — would have been broken.

We know that the Covenant with David concerned the establishment of David's House, which was symbolized by the Cedar. One clue for tracing the Royal House of David is found in the riddles of Ezekiel Chap. 17.

Ezek. 17 vv. 3,4 states, *"A great eagle with great wings, long-winged, full of feathers, which had divers colours, came into Lebanon, and took the highest branch of the cedar. He cropped off the tops of this young twigs, and carried it into a land of traffick: he set it in a city of merchants."* This prophecy was fulfilled when Nebuchadnezzar carried off King Zedekiah (the highest branch) to Babylon, where he died, blinded, in prison.

A further moving is found in verse 22 *"I will also take of the highest branch of the high cedar, and will set it: I will crop off from the top of his young twigs a tender one, and will plant it upon an high mountain and eminent."* This was fulfilled when Scota, King Zedekiah's daughter, (the tender twig) was taken to Egypt by Jeremiah and then to Spain where she married "ane Greyk callit Gathelus, son of Cecrops of Athens, King of Argives." (The Chronicles of Scotland by Hector Boece) In due time a son was born and was named "Eochaidh." (Eremhon or King)

There is a tradition that when Jeremiah brought Scota to Spain, he also brought the "stone" upon which Jacob laid his head, at Bethel, when he had the vision of a ladder extending to heaven. (Gen. 28:12-19) This was the "stone" used as a Coronation Stone in Solomon's Temple. II Kings 11:11-14 tells of the annointing of a king, after which all the men around the king *"clapped their hands"* and said, *"God save the King"* while *"the king stood by a pillar, as the manner was, and the princes and the trumpeters by the king."*

From the "Annals of the Kingdom of Ireland by the Four Masters," we find the following statement: "Tea, the daughter of Loghaldh, son of Ith, whom Eremhon married in Spain was the Tea who requested of Eremhon a choice hill as her dower, in whatever place she should select it, that she might be interred therein. The hill she selected was Druim-caein, i.e. Teamhair (in Ireland)." (Vol. 1, pg. 31)

This is only one of many historical records that place not only Tea in Ireland, but her husband Eochaidh, "the Heremon." (chief or King) At this same time there appeared, with Eochaidh (brought by Dedannans and set up at Tara as the inauguration stone of Irish Kings – Encyclopedia Britannica 14th ed.) a stone of red sandstone, a type found in Palestine. It had iron rings fastened at each end which could have been used for porter poles. The stone became known by the name "Lia Fail" and "Stone of Destiny." It is not unlikely that Jacob's Stone and the "Stone of Destiny" were one and the same.

From Ireland, the Stone and the Throne were removed to Scotland, by Fergus the Great, as he was crowned King of Scotland. For hundreds of years all the Scottish Kings were crowned upon the "Stone of Destiny." In the year 1296 A.D. Edward the First removed the Stone to England for his crowning as King of the United Kingdom of Scotland and England.

Today, the Stone rests under the famous Coronation Throne in Westminster Abbey. All the Kings and Queens of Britain, except one, have been crowned over the "Stone of Destiny." The last monarch, Queen Elizabeth herself, a direct descendant of David, was crowned upon the Stone in 1953; in fulfillment of God's Covenant with David that as long as the sun, moon and stars continue in the heavens, (Jer. 31:35) the House and Throne of David would continue, till He comes whose right it is to reign. (Psalms 89:34-37; Luke 1:32)

(For more complete details of the story of David's Throne and the Stone of Destiny, read "Jacob's Pillar" – by Capt – see listing inside rear cover.)

THE APPOINTED PLACE

"For the Lord shall smite Israel as a reed is shaken in the water, and he shall root up Israel out of this good land, which he gave to their fathers, and shall scatter them beyond the River (Euphrates), because they have made their groves (idolatrous symbols) provoking the Lord to anger" (I Kings 14:15).

After the death of Solomon, the kingdom of Israel was divided into two nations. The tribes of Judah and Benjamin formed the Southern Kingdom of Judah and the other ten tribes formed the Northern Kingdom of Israel.

Because of their continued sinning, by worshipping idols, God caused His people Israel to be removed from their homeland. II Kings 15:29; 17:6,7; 18:11,12, record how the Assyrians carried off the Northern Kingdom of Israel to Assyria. II Kings 18:13 states how the Assyrians also carried off most of the Southern Kingdom of Judah to Assyria, leaving only the inhabitants of the city of Jerusalem. (II Kings 19:31-36) They, in turn, were taken by Nebuchadnezzar, to Babylonian Captivity. Only a remnant of these people eventually made their way back to Jerusalem, some 50 years later, to begin rebuilding the Temple, under Zerubbabel.

This is where many Biblical scholars fail to fully understand the Scriptures. They declare that because God had caused Israel to be driven from the land of Palestine, He had cast them away forever. In doing so, God had brought His Kingdom, established at Mount Sinai, to an end and in its place had chosen what they term the "Gentile Church" or "Spiritual Israel."

If God cast His people away forever and they no longer exist as a people then God has lied. He has been unfaithful, He has broken His Covenant with them and is not dependable. In contradiction to this theory, God is faithful. He cannot and will not lie (Heb. 6:18) and He will keep His Covenant with them.

No proof can be found, in the Scriptures, that God has cast away His people, forever. Even in Leviticus Chap. 26, where God warned Israel that the result of their continued sinning would be their removal from their land, He added (in the 44th verse) the definite statement that even when they were in the hands of their enemies He would not cast them away. He would remember His Covenant. (Abrahamic Covenant) This is repeated in Deut. 4:26-31.

In Isaiah 41:8,9, after all Israel had been scattered, God says He has not cast them away. In Amos 9:9 God says: *"For, lo, I will command, and I will sift the house of Israel among all nations, like as corn is sifted in a sieve, yet shall not the least grain fall upon the earth.''* Then in vs. 14,15, God promises to bring His people Israel to their appointed land where they *"shall no more be pulled up out of their land which I have given them.''*

In Ezekiel 34:1-16, God sees His sheep, His people Israel, "scattered upon all the face of the earth," as lost sheep without a shepherd, and in the 11th and 12th verses, *"For thus saith the Lord God, Behold I, even I, will both search my sheep, and seek them out, as a shepherd seeketh out his flock in the day that he is among his sheep...and will deliver them out of all places where they have been scattered in the cloudy and dark day.''*

In Jeremiah 18, God tells the prophet that just as the potter's clay was "marred" in the hands of the potter, but taken again the second time and remoulded into a perfect vessel, so would He do with the House of Israel.

In Jer. 23, God states: *"and I will gather the remnant of my flock out of all countries whither I have driven them, and will bring them again to their folds; and they shall be fruitful and increase''* (Jer. 23:3) and *"But, the Lord liveth, which brought up and which led the seed of the House of Israel out of the north country, and from all countries whither I had driven them; and they shall dwell in their own land.''* (Jer. 23:8)

Again, in Jer. 46:27, God told Israel He would save them from

84

"afar off" together with all their seed. And in Ezekiel 20:34, God promised to gather Israel out of the countries wherein they were "scattered." Then, in the closing book of the Old Testament, Malachi 3:6, God says to Israel, *"I am the Lord, I change not, therefore ye sons of Jacob are NOT consumed."*

We also find in the New Testament when Christ, the God of Israel, came to earth He declared, *"I am not sent, but unto the lost sheep of the House of Israel"* (Matt. 15:24). Would He have come to seek a people that did not exist? Rather, it is declared of Him that He came to *"confirm the promises made unto the fathers."* (Rom. 15:8)

Also, Paul in answer to the question, *"Hath God cast away His people?"* replied in no uncertain terms, *"God hath NOT cast away His people."* (Rom. 11:1,2) There are other scriptures to be found that also prove God has sworn He will never cast them away, nor break His Everlasting Covenant with them.

Our Lord Jesus Christ, Paul, Peter, James and the prophets all declare they are NOT cast away, but many theologians teach that God has cast them away forever, thereby nullifying His Everlasting Covenant with them. Whem do you believe? If you really believe God, then there can be only one answer, and that is the answer given by Paul, *"God hath not cast away His people."* What then has become of them? Where is the appointed place God promised the people, for a new homeland?

Many clues to the "appointed place" are given in the Scriptures: *"Hear the word of the Lord, O ye nations, and declare it in the isles afar off and say, He that scattered Israel will gather him and keep him, as a shepherd doth his flock."* (Jer. 31:10) Isaiah also addresses many of his prophecies to Israel *"in the Isles,"* such as Chapter 24:14,15: *"They shall lift up their voice, they shall sing for the majesty of the Lord, they shall cry aloud from the sea. Wherefore glorify ye the Lord in the fires, even the name of the Lord God of Israel in the isles of the sea."*

Here, the Hebrew word "zam" is translated as "sea," but it can also translate to "west" meaning a point on the compass. Therefore, the verse could read *"the isles of the west."*

Then, in Isaiah 42: v. 4, we find: *"He shall not fail nor be discouraged, till he have set judgment in the earth; and the isles shall wait for his law."* And v. 12 reads: *"Let them give glory unto the Lord, and declare his praise in the islands."* Again, Chap. 49 v. 1 says: *"Listen O Isles unto me."*

Isaiah 59:18,19 states, *"To the islands he will repay recompense.*

So shall they fear the name of the Lord from the west." Thus we see the Scriptures plainly show that the "appointed" land includes some islands and Isaiah places them "west" of Palestine.

From Jeremiah we learn that these islands are not only in the west but in the *Northwest.* The word sent to Israel by Jeremiah is sent to the *north: "Go and proclaim these words toward the north, and say, 'Return thou backsliding Israel'.* " (Jer. 3:12)

The Scriptures also tell us that the "appointed" place is associated with the *wilderness.*" Hosea, who foretold of Israel's captivity, tells of God "alluring" Israel and bringing her *"into the wilderness"* and speaking *"comfortably unto her.*" (Hosea 2:14) Then there follows a description of the *"wilderness"* and the blessings that God will bestow upon Israel.

Jeremiah speaks of the *"wilderness"* as the place where, *"the people which were left of the sword found grace."* and affirms the identity of the people by adding, *"even Israel, when I went to cause him to rest."* (Jer. 31:2)

The *wilderness* is also spoken of by the prophet Ezekiel, as the place God would bring His people after His fury had been poured out upon them; *"And I will bring you out from the people, and will gather you out of the countries wherein ye are scattered, with a mighty hand, and with a stretched out arm, and with fury poured out. And I will bring you into the wilderness of the people, and there will I plead with you face to face."* (Ezek. 20:34,35)

This closely resembles the *"alluring"* into the wilderness as prophesied by Hosea and Jeremiah. It is evident that Ezekiel's *"wilderness"* and that prophesied by Hosea and Jeremiah refer to one and the same place.

One hears it constantly asserted by students of Bible prophecy that, "Israel is to be restored to the Promised Land in unbelief." Here is an example of how failure to distinguish between different appelations brings confusion and misunderstandings.

If by "Israel," they mean only the "Nation of the Jews" that was established after 538 B.C., when Cyrus destroyed the Babylonian Empire; a nation composed of the remnant of Judah, Benjamin, Levi with Babylonians (who fled to Jerusalem with the Judeans) and Edomites (who had occupied the land during the captivity period) then they are perfectly correct. A certain portion of this group is prophesied to return to Palestine, in unbelief.

But if they mean the whole of the 12 tribes of Israel, then they are quite mistaken. Israel was promised a *"place of their own"* where they shall *"move no more."* (II Sam. 7:10) Any restoration of Israel as a whole, to the Promised Land, by representation or otherwise, can only come AFTER they have first become a Christian people: are *"sons of the Living God,"* (Hosea 1:10) have *"found grace in the wilderness,"* (Jer. 31:2) and are brought into *"the Bond of the Covenant."* (Ezek. 20:37)

Another clue to the direction of the "appointed" land from Palestine is found in Isaiah: *"Listen, O isles, unto Me: and hearken ye people from far."* (Isa. 49:1) In verse 12, Isaiah, referring to a future millennial return of Israel from the isles to Palestine, states; *"Behold these shall come from far; and lo these from the north and from the west: and these from the land of Sinim."* Not only is the location *"from afar,"* but clearly indicates the *Northwest.* In Hebrew there is no one word for northwest, it has to be expressed by the words "the north and the west."

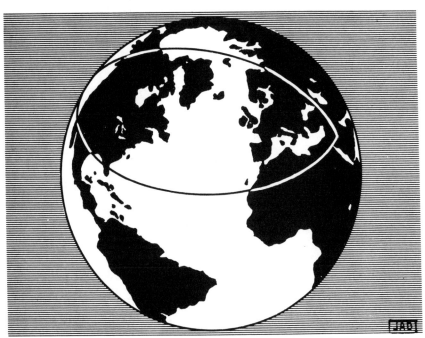

"Fully accomplished were the words of Isaiah"

These words were written by Columbus to King Ferdinand of Spain, in 1502, acknowledging Isaiah's prophecies of Israel's dispersal.

MIGRATIONS OF ISRAEL

"In the ninth year of Hoshea, the king of Assyria took Samaria, and carried Israel away into Assyria, and placed them in Halah, and in Habor by the river of Gozan, and in the cities of the Medes." (II Kings 17:6)

The first archaeological evidence to establish a chronological link in the contacts between Assyria and Israel are found on inscriptions on the side of a limestone stele found at Nimrud, known as the "Black Obelisk." The stone was inscribed with the records of Shalmaneser III and an illustration of the Israelite king Jehu bringing tribute to the Assyrian king. An inscription above the illustration says: "This is Jehu (Iaua), the son of Khumri. (Omri)"

Omri in Hebrew begins with the consonant, "Agin," formerly called "Gayin" which was pronounced with a gutteral "H," that is "Gh" or "Kh." The Israelites would have naturally pronounced Omri as "Ghomri" which became "Khumri" in Assyrian.

As this inscription was executed nearly a century before the captivity of Israel, we know now the reason secular historians found no mention of the exiled Israelites in ancient records. It was simply because the Assyrians who took the Israelites captive did not call them by that name.

The next archaelogical evidence, directly related to the Israelites movements in Assyria, was found in the form of cuneiform writings on a collection of clay tablets. They were found nearly a century ago in the excavations of Nineveh, and published in 1930. (The Royal Correspondence of the Assyrian Empire by L. Waterman) Their relevance to Israel was overlooked till recently because of their being in complete disorder, among some 1400 other texts.

The first of the documents were Assyrian frontier post reports of 707 B.C. They reported that the armed forces of Urartu (Ararat) were invading the district south of Lake Urmia, in Media, where the Israelites had been placed some 14 years earlier.

The reports went on to say that when the king of Urartu came into the land of "Gamir," the army was routed as the "Gamera" counterattacked, entered the land of Urartu and killed their commanders. All historians agree that the "Gamera" were the same people who, thirty years later, in the reign of Esarhaddon (the Assyrian king) were called "Gimira." Gamir is evidently a corruption of Ghomri, formed by the inversion of the final syllable -ri to -ir. Such inversions are common in Assyrian writings.

Another and later Assyrian tablet recorded that in the 2nd year of Esarhaddon the king (about 679 B.C.) the Gimira under their leader Teuspa, sought freedom by moving north, but the Assyrian army pursued and defeated them in the upper Euphrates district. Nevertheless large numbers of the Israelites escaped to the shores of the Black Sea. The Greek records refer to these Gimira as "Kimmeroii" which is translated into English as "Cimmerian."

The Greek Geographer Strabo informs us the Cimmerians captured the kingdom of Phrygia about 695 B.C. Later, they twice invaded Lydia, the second time successfully, and occupied Sardis the capital (662 B.C.). About 600 B.C. the Lydians drove the Cimmerians out of Asia Minor altogether, and they crossed the Black Sea and entered the Carpathian regions, called (in 2nd Esdras) Ar-sareth, or Mountains of Sereth.

The main body of Israelites in Media accepted an alliance with Esarhaddon. At this time the Assyrians were under attack by both the Medes and Babylonians. The new alliance allowed the Israelites to establish colonies in Sacasene in the north and Bactria in the east.

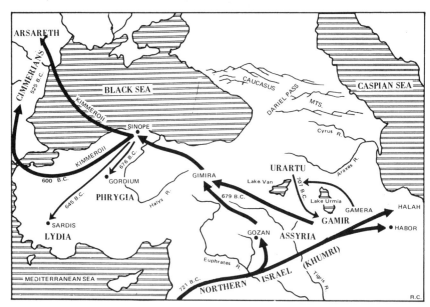

Israel — Khumri — Gamera — Gimera — Kimmeroii — Cimmerians

When Assyria fell in 612 B.C. to the Medes and Babylonians, the two colonies came under pressure from the Medes. The main body of Israelites in Sacasene, west of the Caspian Sea, crossed the Araxes River (passing northward through the Dariel Pass in the Caucasus)

90

and occupied the steppe regions of South Russia. There they became known by the Greek name "Scythians."

Those that had settled east in Bactria migrated still further east into Central Asia, some even as far as the borders of China. Most of our history of this eastern division of Israelites is found in Persian inscriptions which refer to the Israelites as "Saka" or "Sacae."

The Assyrians called these colonies Gimira, but later "Iskuza," a name which may have been derived from Isaaca, or house of Isaac, the name which the Israelites called themselves. (Amos 7:9,16)

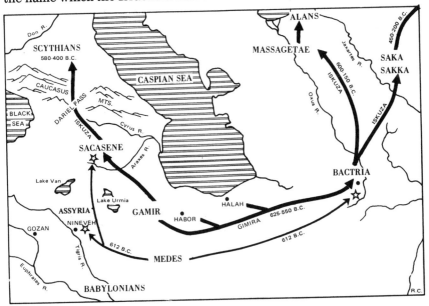

(Israel - Khumri) - Gimira - Iskuza - Scythians - Saka - Massagetae

In the famous Behistun Rock tri-lingual inscriptions of Darius I (522-485 B.C.) the name Saka in the Persian and Elamite inscriptions is rendered Gimira in the Babylonian version.

Following the fall of Nineveh in 612 B.C. the Assyrian Empire was split between the conquering Medes and Babylonians. The Medes took over the territory to the north and northwest, while the Babylonians assumed control over the lands to the south and southwest.

Babylon, under King Nebuchadnezzar quickly assumed the conquest of Judah. In a series of invasions, against the Southern Kingdom of Judah, he captured and deported remnants of Israelites missed by the Assyrians. Finally moving against Jerusalem, he fulfilled God's prophecy against Israel by capturing the city and taking the balance of the Nation of Judah to Babylon.

In 539 B.C., when Cyrus, King of Persia overthrew the Babylonian Empire, he permitted the remnant of Judah to return to Jerusalem. He also offered freedom for any of the Babylonians who wished to migrate with these Israelites.

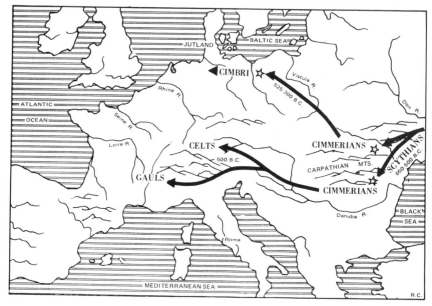

Cimmerians — Celtic tribes

Between 539 and 500 B.C., during the rebuilding of the Temple, the Scythian "Israelites," who had been pushed north through the Dariel Pass, began to move westward, crossing the rivers Don and Dnieper, thus coming into collision with the Cimmerian Israelites who had earlier migrated around the west of the Black Sea. The Cimmerians were consequently driven north and west. A small group north of the Carpathian Mountains moved into the sparsely inhabited regions of the Baltic, where the Romans called them by the abbreviated name of Cimbri. The main body south of the Carpathian Mountains migrated as scattered bands up the River Danube arriving, near its source, in south Germany between 500 and 450 B.C. There they became known as Celts and Gauls.

By the end of the 4th century B.C., the Scythian "Israelites," who had established themselves in South Russia as the great and prosperous kingdom of Scythia, came under attack by a mixed non-Israelitish people of Iranian origin, called "Sarmations." The Scythians were driven north toward the Baltic regions, pushing the Cimri ahead of them, west to Jutland and the coasts of Holland and France.

92

As the Celts spread west and north across France, during the great Celtic expansion from Europe, some moved across the English Channel into Britain. About 390 B.C. one group invaded Italy and sacked Rome. Around 280 B.C. others reached Greece, and as they migrated back into Asia Minor, the Greeks called them "Galations." This would indicate that Paul's letters to the "Galations," were to his kindred Israelites.

As the Sarmation tribes now occupied "Scythia" in South Russia, there was a tendency to confuse them with the Scythians, but the Romans came up with a solution to that problem. They introduced the name "German" for the genuine "Scythian;" "Germanus" being the Latin word for "genuine." Except for the outlaying districts, the name "Scythians" was dropped, in the Roman records, in favor of "Germans" and "Sarmations."

The Cimbri were finally driven out of their area by the "German" Scythians. Only a residue of one group reached Spain, whereas the main body reached Italy only to be almost entirely wiped out by the Roman legions. A few Cimbri did escape, by boat, to northern Britain to become the Picts.

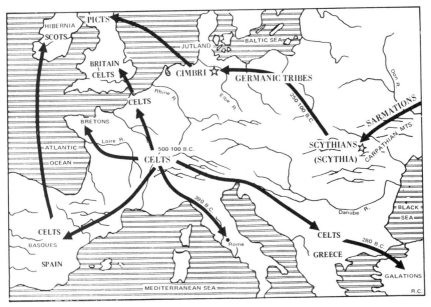

Israel Peoples

The Celts continued to pour into Britain to form the "bed-rock" of the British race. One group in Spain, known as "Iberes," the Gaelic name for Hebrews, moved into Ireland as Scots, naming the island Hibernia, a name that still exists. Those remaining in Spain

93

became known as Basques; others, in France, became known as Bretons.

During the succeeding centuries the Scythian Germans broke up into many divisions, possibly in some instances into their original Israel tribal families. One group split off and formed the Goths, settling around the shores of the Baltic Sea. Others became the Angles, Saxons, Jutes, Danes and Vikings; to name just a few. Then, other Germanic tribes poured into the lands vacated by the Celts and established the Gothic nations of the Vandals, Lombards, Franks, Burgundians and Ostrogoths.

Between 450 and 600 A.D., some of the Angles and Saxons moved into Britain as Anglo-Saxons. Between 850 and 1000 A.D. the Danes and Vikings raided the coasts of Britain, establishing some colonies, while others settled in Iceland and Greenland. One group moved into France as Normans.

The Celtic Scots of Ireland, for the most part, moved into northern Britain and established the Nation of Scotland.

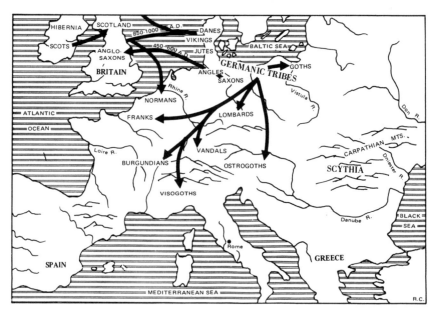

Sythians — Germanic tribes

In this "synopsis" we have not attempted to present all the details of the migrations of the people known as "Cimmerians" and "Scythians." This can be found in your libraries on detailed maps, produced by historians and archaeologists. It is the ORIGIN of the Cimmerians

94

and the Scythians, who formed the Anglo-Saxon, Scandinavian, Germanic, Lombardic and Celtic nations, that has not been known until now.

One of the greatest mysteries of Archaeology is where the countless thousands of Scythians and Cimmerians came from. Did they just "materialize," leaving no evidence of where they originated?

One of the greatest mysteries of the Bible is what happened to the countless thousands of Israelites who disappeared from history, south of the Caucasus, at the same time the Scythians and Cimmerians "appeared."

There is no longer any "mystery." They were one and the same people. And thus, we see the fulfillment of God's Covenant with the people of David's kingdom as they migrated to their "appointed" place: to western Europe, to the Isles in the west, and then on to America, the land in the "wilderness," where we have been, as was prophesied of the House of Israel, "Blind" to our Identity. (Rom. 11:25)

Our God, the Supreme architect of the Universe, is a Covenant keeping God. He fulfilled His promise that said; *He that scattered Israel will gather him, and keep him, as a shepherd doth his flock."* (Jer. 31:10) We thus can be assured that He who guides us, His people Israel, and performs all that He has promised to us, will certainly — Save – Keep – and Bless all those who put their trust in Him.

I hope this booklet has given you, the reader, a closer relationship with God, the "Master Builder" and His Son Jesus Christ, the "Lord of the True Temple," as you see fulfilled, some of the revealed symbolism of King Solomon's Temple.

Knowledge of this fulfillment is necessary to fully understand the wonderful truths God directed Solomon to incorporate in the design of the Temple.

Such knowledge is required, to complete the Divine purpose for which each of us was ordained to become: "a kingdom of priests, and an holy nation," (Exod. 19:6) so as to take our places in the True Temple, in the impending "Kingdom of God" upon earth.

ACKNOWLEDGEMENT

This treatise is indebted to the Palestine Exploration Society and other past Bible historians and archaeologists, whose dedicated labors have provided the foundation on which we can build a better understanding of the description, given in sacred history, of Solomon's Temple.

Artist sketches of the basic design of the Temple as well as the "Molten Sea," used in this treatise, were suggested by the "Howland-Garber Model Reconstruction of Solomon's Temple." Deviations from this design concept have been made, based on modern Bible interpretations and practicality of application.

The archaeological evidence of the migrations of Israel is derived from the cuneiform tablets of the "Royal Correspondence of the Assyrian Empire" - translated by Professor Leroy Waterman of the University of Michigan - 1930. A detailed account of the captivity and subsequent migrations of the tribes of Israel, supplemented by historical research, is available in the publication, "Missing Links Discovered in Assyrian Tablets" (Capt - Artisan Sales - 1985 - 256 pages with over 100 illustrations and charts).

Much more research and study is necessary before every facet of this wonderful Temple's symbolism shines forth, in all its perfection. This remains to be done by honest and sincere searchers for truth, who will produce more of that which we so earnestly desire; LIGHT for our time.

E. Raymond Capt

> "Our eyes are holden that we cannot see things that stare us in the face until the hour arrives when the mind is ripened. Then we behold them, and the time when we saw them not is like a dream."
>
> (R. W. Emerson)